Contents

W9-CZT-370

Nearly two thousand years ago the words of the Prophets came true. A baby was born to a carpenter and his wife in a stable in Bethlehem. He was the long awaited Messiah, the Son of God, and was named Jesus.

Through simple, meaningful language enhanced by incomparable colour illustrations, this New Testament tells the story of the life and work of Jesus and the birth of the world-wide Christian church.

© LADYBIRD BOOKS LTD MCMLXXXI

Script copyright 'God's Story' © Yorkshire Television MCMLXXX
Text © Scripture Union MCMLXXXI
Illustrations © Scripture Union MCMLXXX

First published 1981 by Scripture Union,
130 City Road, London, EC1V-2NJ   ISBN 0 85421 9048
and Ladybird Books Limited, Loughborough, Leics.   ISBN 0 7214 7518 3

Library of Congress Cataloging in Publication Data

Robertson, Jenny.
    The Ladybird New Testament.

    Summary: A collection of stories from the New Testament from the birth of Jesus through the work of the Apostles, retold with illustrations.
    1. Bible stories, English—N.T.   [1. Bible stories—N.T.]   I. Parry, Alan, ill.   II. Title.
BS2401.R52   225.9'505   81-13061
ISBN 0-310-44450-0   AACR2

First Zondervan printing 1982

Printed in the United States of America

The Ladybird
New Testament

Text by
JENNY ROBERTSON
based on the 'God's Story'
script by Oliver Hunkin,
in association with
Yorkshire Television.

Illustrated by
ALAN PARRY

Ladybird Books Loughborough

JESUS THE CHILD

Mary and the angel

This is the story of Jesus and the first of his followers. It began nearly two thousand years ago in Nazareth, a little village in the land of Israel. A young woman named Mary was getting the dinner ready. Beans and yellow peas bubbled in the pot on the stove, and Mary was mixing dough for the barley bread. It seemed just like any other evening.

Suddenly a voice called her name. She looked up amazed; a stranger stood beside her. Light shone from his face, even his clothes seemed full of light. He was an angel sent from God.

'The Lord is with you, Mary,' the angel said. 'He is pleased with you. He will make a baby grow inside you; a little boy whose name is to be Jesus. He is God's own Son, the promised king who will save his people from the wrongdoing and wickedness that keep them from knowing God.'

At first Mary did not understand the angel, then she said, 'I am the Lord's servant. I will do whatever he wants.'

Mary and Joseph

Mary was going to be married to a man called Joseph who was the village carpenter. When he heard about the baby, Joseph thought he should not marry Mary after all. Then an angel spoke to him in a dream and told him that God had sent the baby to Mary. The angel

told Joseph to marry her, and Joseph believed the angel and did as he said.

The journey to Bethlehem

One day, soon after their wedding, Joseph said to Mary, 'I have some news for you, dear. Our rulers, the Romans, have ordered everyone to go back to the towns where they were born, to have their names put on a register. They are trying to count everyone in our country so that they can tax them. My family comes from Bethlehem so we must go there. I'm afraid it will be a hard journey for you,' added Joseph, anxiously.

'God will look after us,' said Mary quietly. She knew that the Romans could not be disobeyed. Their soldiers had conquered Israel, and their Emperor ruled the land.

So they set off. Soon they joined other travellers, all making their way across the rocky countryside to Bethlehem. At night they camped by the roadside, sleeping on the ground with only a fire to keep the wild beasts away. Then, at last, Joseph pointed to a little walled town on a hillside ahead.

'There we are, nearly there now!' he said.

'I shall be glad to get to an inn,' said Mary. 'I can feel that my baby will be born soon!'

'Then we must hurry! Bethlehem is the town where King David was born, hundreds of years ago. Our teachers have often told us that another special leader will

be born in Bethlehem. He is the one who will guide our people in God's ways.'

'Hurry, little donkey!' said Mary. 'The teachers were right. Our baby king, Jesus, will be born tonight in Bethlehem. God is watching over us!'

In the stable

The streets of Bethlehem were crowded with tired travellers.

'I have no room anywhere. We're packed out!' cried the innkeeper.

'Please,' Mary begged, 'my baby will be born very soon. Can't you help at all?'

'I wish I could, dear!' the innkeeper answered. 'Wait a minute, though . . . you can sleep in the stable! The straw's clean enough, and the cows will keep you warm. Look – this way . . .'

The stable was little more than a cave, but later that night, Jesus, God's own Son was born there, and Mary laid him in a manger filled with hay, because there was no room for him in the busy inn.

The shepherds' king

No one in the crowded town knew that the promised king was lying asleep in the stable, but an angel told the news to some shepherds who were looking after their sheep in the fields outside Bethlehem.

'News! Good news for everyone!' The shepherds looked up, terrified. A great company of angels, brighter than the starlit sky, crowded round them.

'Don't be afraid,' said one. 'Your promised king, your Saviour Christ the Lord, has been born close by in Bethlehem. You'll find him there, wrapped in linen cloths,

lying in a manger. Go quickly and see!'

Then the shepherds heard the angels singing, 'Glory to the most high God! Peace to his people on earth!'

They left their sheep and hurried up the hill to Bethlehem.

Trying not to make too much noise, they crowded into the stable and knelt beside the manger where Jesus slept on the hay.

When they saw the tiny baby, they whispered joyfully, 'O, praise God! Thank God! He has sent this little one to be our Saviour. The promised king has been born in a stable, not in a rich palace. God has not forgotten us, his poor people!'

The shepherds hurried away, still praising God. Mary sat and watched her baby boy.

'It's dark in the stable. The cows moo and stamp. Rats rustle in the hay, but the music of highest heaven plays for you, dear Jesus. Sleep well, little one, sleep well,' Mary murmured.

The wise men

Far away in the desert, wise men were riding towards Bethlehem, following a huge star that blazed in the sky. Each dry hot day they rested, shaded by their kneeling camels, but at night they rode on, following the star. The cold wind stung their faces as they gazed at the sky.

'The star tells me that a king is born,' said one. 'I am old, yet when I saw the star I left my home and my books to follow it and find the king.'

'It must be guiding us to a royal palace. Surely that is where we shall find such an important baby!' said another.

So when they came to the city of Jerusalem, where the royal palace of Israel was, they went no further, but stopped to look for the baby.

The king who lived there was called Herod. He welcomed the wise men, but their news alarmed him.

'A star tells these visitors that a new king has been born in my kingdom!' he thought angrily. 'There's only room for one king in this country, and that's me!'

He turned to the priests who stood near him. 'Where is the promised king to be born?' he asked.

'In Bethlehem, O King!' they answered, bowing low.

'I must get rid of this baby!' thought Herod, and he made a cunning plan.

'Search for the child in Bethlehem,' he told the wise men. 'When you find him, let me know. I want to worship him, too.'

Herod was lying. Really he wanted to kill the baby.

The wise men found Mary and Joseph and the baby in Bethlehem. They knelt and worshipped Jesus. They had brought gifts for him — bright gold, sweet-smelling myrrh and frankincense.

Then God warned the wise men not to trust King Herod. So they did not tell him where Jesus was, but made their way home without going back to Jerusalem.

Escape to Egypt

That night an angel came to Joseph in a dream.

'Herod is looking for the baby to kill him,' said the angel. 'Get up quickly, take baby Jesus and Mary and go to Egypt. Stay there until I tell you to leave.'

So Joseph woke Mary and the baby, and the family escaped from the town.

'I heard the sound of children crying when we crept out of Bethlehem,' said Mary as she followed Joseph along the road.

'I heard it, too,' said Joseph. 'Herod's soldiers are killing all the baby boys in the town. He wanted to kill our baby king. That's why God has told us to escape to the land of Egypt.'

So the little family lived in Egypt until King Herod died and it was safe for them to go back home to Nazareth.

The boy Jesus

In Nazareth the boy Jesus grew up, sturdy and strong. He used to help Joseph in the carpenter's shop. No one in the village knew about the angels who had sung when he was born in Bethlehem, or about the star and the wise men with their costly gifts. Only Mary would sometimes watch her son and wonder what would happen to him.

Then, when Jesus was twelve, he went with his parents to Jerusalem for the great Passover festival. It was wonderful to climb the steep narrow streets to the golden temple! Long after the other families from Nazareth had gone home, Jesus stayed on. He spoke to the wise teachers who taught the people about God.

'Who is this boy?' the learned men wondered. 'He seems to know God in such a special way. He is completely at home here in God's house.'

Meanwhile Joseph and Mary were travelling back to Nazareth. They supposed that Jesus was with them, somewhere in the party of friends and relations. They had made a whole day's journey before they noticed that Jesus was missing. They went all the way back to Jerusalem, looking for him.

At last they found him in the temple.

'Why have you done this to us?' Mary asked. 'We've been so worried about you, we've been looking for you everywhere!'

'Didn't you expect to find me here, in my Father's house?' Jesus answered, but he went quietly home with his parents.

Mary did not understand what he meant then, but she often thought about his words. When Jesus grew up and started to do the special work that God, his Father, had planned for him, she remembered and understood.

JESUS BEGINS HIS SPECIAL WORK

John the Baptist

So the years passed by until at last it was nearly time for Jesus to put away his carpenter's tools and go to do the special work which God had planned for him.

At about this time Jesus' cousin John left his home and went to live in the desert beyond the River Jordan. He wore rough clothes made from camel hair and ate the food of the desert: locusts — creatures like large grasshoppers — and wild honey.

Every day John would stand by the banks of the river and teach the people about God. His eyes glowed like the hot sun and his voice, strong as the desert wind, drew large crowds who flocked to hear John's news about the king that God was going to send.

'You are all doing wrong things, things that make God angry,' John cried. 'You must stop, and start to lead good lives so that God can forgive you. I will baptise you here in the Jordan as a sign that you are sorry. There isn't much time! We know that God promised to give us a special king to lead us. He will come soon, and we must be ready for him!'

One day Jesus came to the river and asked John to baptise him, too. John knew at once that Jesus was God's promised king. At first he did not want to baptise Jesus, but Jesus knew that this was what God wanted, even though he had done nothing wrong. So humbly, John baptised him.

As they came up from the water they heard the voice of God himself saying, 'This is my own dear Son. I am very pleased with him.'

Jesus in the desert

Then Jesus left the crowds on the river bank and went by himself into the desert. There was nowhere for him to shelter from the scorching midday sun or the cold wind that blew at night. Wild animals roamed across the sands and evil lurked there.

When Jesus had been alone for forty days the Devil came to test him. He wanted Jesus to use the power he had as God's Son to win

praise for himself instead of carrying out God's work. The Devil knew that Jesus had no food to eat, so first of all he tried to persuade him to turn the desert stones into bread. Jesus refused.

'People need more than bread to stay alive,' he told the Devil. 'They need to know the words of God, and to obey them, too.'

The Devil tried again. He took Jesus to the highest tower of the temple in Jerusalem.

'Jump down!' he said. 'Don't be afraid! You won't hurt yourself. The holy writings teach that God will send his angels to catch you!'

'The holy writings also say that we must not try to test God!' Jesus replied.

Then the Devil showed Jesus the kingdoms of the world with all their power and wealth.

'I will give all this to you if you will just kneel down and worship me!' the Devil said.

'Go away, Devil!' Jesus answered, sternly. 'God is the only one we should worship.'

Defeated, the Devil left him alone, and God sent angels to strengthen him after his test.

Now Jesus was ready to go back to the people who lived in the towns and villages round about and teach them about God.

Jesus goes to a wedding

One day Jesus and some of his friends were invited to a wedding with Mary, Jesus' mother. Everyone enjoyed the party afterwards, but after a while Mary's friend came over to her.

'What shall we do?' she asked. 'We've run out of wine!'

It was a disgrace not to be able to offer wine to the guests all through the wedding party. Mary felt sorry for her friend. She told Jesus what had happened. Then she spoke to the servants. 'My son Jesus will help. Just do whatever he tells you!'

There were six huge jars standing near the door. Jesus told the servants to fill them with water.

'Now take some out and give it to the best man,' he said, when the jars were full.

One of the servants filled a jug. He waited anxiously while the best man drank. Would he be angry at being offered water? But the best man smiled.

'This is the best wine I have ever tasted; fancy saving it until last!' he exclaimed.

Jesus had turned all the water into wine! Now everyone could enjoy the celebrations.

Jesus calls the fishermen

Not far from the town where the wedding was held lay a large lake called the Sea of Galilee. One afternoon two fishermen sat mending their nets on the shore where the fishing boats were beached. Their names were Peter and Andrew.

Two children came by and stopped to watch.

'Jesus is coming this way,' the children said. 'We saw him back there along the shore.'

Simon and Andrew looked up quickly. Simon had met Jesus before, and he wanted to talk to him again.

Then they saw Jesus in the distance, calling them.

'Simon! Andrew! Leave your nets! Come with me! I want you to help me to tell everyone about God!'

At once the fishermen leapt to their feet. They waved goodbye to the children and set off after Jesus.

Further up the beach two more fishermen, called James and John, were working in their boat with their father. They were cousins of Jesus, like John who had baptised him.

'Come with us,' Jesus called to them. 'I need your help, too.' So the two men said goodbye to their father and went with Jesus.

Jesus makes the sick well

Simon, who was also known as Peter, invited them all to come home with him.

'My wife and her mother will be so pleased to see you, Jesus!' he said.

Simon Peter did not know that his wife's mother was ill. They found her in bed.

'Oh, dear Teacher,' she said when she saw Jesus, 'I would like to have given you a proper welcome, but then I felt so hot and weak I had to lie down . . .'

Jesus bent down and touched the old woman's hand. She felt better immediately. In fact, she got up at once and cooked them a delicious meal.

That evening crowds of sick people gathered outside Simon's house. Those who couldn't walk were carried by their friends. Children led their elderly, ailing grandparents, mothers brought their sick babies, and blind people were guided there. People who were possessed by evil spirits, and sad people, whose worries made them ill, came too. Jesus helped them all. He touched the sick and made them well. He drove away the evil spirits. Everyone discovered that God cared about them and had sent Jesus to help them, and make them well again.

Jesus and a lame man

More and more people wanted Jesus to heal their sick friends and relatives. One day four men brought a lame friend to the house where Jesus was staying. Their friend had been lame for twenty years. He couldn't walk at all, and his friends had to carry him on a mattress. When they reached the house they couldn't get in because of the crowds round the door. So they went up on to the roof, which was flat and made of mud, and began to scrape a hole large enough to let their friend through. The mud crumbled away easily, and soon they could lower their friend down to Jesus.

Jesus looked at the man and said, 'Everything you've done wrong is forgiven. Now you will be able to get up and walk.'

Some of the Jewish leaders, the priests and scribes who taught the people about God and his laws, were standing in the crowd, watching. They were shocked and angry.

'Only God can forgive people like that,' they said. 'Who does Jesus think he is?'

But the man stood up happily. He thanked Jesus and hurried out, running and jumping on his legs that were strong again.

Jesus and a tax-collector

Now Jesus chose someone else to help him – Matthew, the tax-collector. The tax-men collected money from the people to give to their Roman rulers. Nobody liked the Romans, who had taken over Palestine, and they despised the tax-collectors who worked for them. To make matters worse, the tax-collectors often cheated the people, taking money for themselves as well.

No one spoke to tax-collectors unless they had to, but Jesus went straight to the table where Matthew was working.

'Follow me!' he said.

At once Matthew decided to leave his money bags and rolls of accounts. He got to his feet and hurried away with Jesus. That evening he held a party so that other tax-collectors could meet Jesus, too. The Jewish leaders and some of the other bystanders were shocked to see Jesus mixing with such dishonest people, but Jesus explained, 'Bad people need me, too. In fact they are the very ones I have come to help.'

Jesus and Nicodemus

All this puzzled the religious leaders. When Jesus made people well and taught them so wisely it seemed to prove that he came from God. Yet because he mixed with bad people he seemed to be breaking God's holy laws. One of the religious leaders, a man called Nicodemus, was so puzzled that one night after dark, when the city was deserted and there was no one to see, Nicodemus went to find Jesus.

They talked together for a long time. Jesus answered Nicodemus' questions and explained many things to him. At last Nicodemus went home very thoughtfully. He decided to become a follower of Jesus too, but he kept it a secret for a long time.

Jesus and a Samaritan woman

Jesus and his friends used to go round the countryside together, teaching people about God's ways. One hot day they were travelling through a district called Samaria. The others went off to buy food, while Jesus rested beside a well.

A Samaritan woman came by for some water. She didn't speak to Jesus, for Samaritans and Jews were enemies and never spoke to one another. In any case, a Jewish man would not usually speak to a woman if he met her outside her home. To her surprise, however, Jesus asked her for a drink of water.

'Why are you asking me?' she exclaimed. Soon they were deep in conversation. As Jesus talked, the woman's amazement grew. Jesus knew all about her, even about the wrong things she had done, but he still wanted to help her to learn more about God. Greatly impressed, she decided to bring her friends to meet him. Many of them believed Jesus' message about God, and they asked him to stay with them and teach them more. Jesus was only too pleased to agree and he stayed two more days with the Samaritan woman and her friends.

Jesus and his Father

One day Jesus took Peter, James and John into the hills. They climbed a high, lonely mountain and Jesus went ahead to pray. As the fishermen watched they saw his face shining. His clothes dazzled them with a whiteness brighter than snow in sunshine. Jesus stood bathed in light. Two

men stood talking to him. They were Moses and Elijah, two long-dead leaders of the Jewish people. Amazed, Peter called out to Jesus. At that moment a shining cloud covered them, and from it came the voice of God himself: 'This is my dear Son. Listen to him!'

The fishermen fell on their faces in fear. When they dared to look up again, Moses and Elijah had gone. Only Jesus stood beside them, telling them not to be afraid. Slowly they went down the mountain. Now they knew that Jesus really was God's Son, but they still did not understand everything that this meant. They only realised later when Jesus had died and come to life again, as he had said he would. Jesus himself told them to say nothing about what they had seen until that happened.

JESUS THE STORYTELLER

The good shepherd

By now large crowds followed Jesus wherever he went, and he taught them about God. Jesus always spoke simply, and he didn't make things difficult to understand, as their leaders often did. Instead he told them interesting stories. Here are some of the stories that Jesus told.

Once there was a shepherd who looked after his sheep so well he knew exactly which ones belonged to him even when they were in a big sheepfold with lots of other flocks. The shepherd soon sorted out his sheep from the rest. He

knew their names too and he called to each one. The sheep understood because they recognized their shepherd's voice. They followed him as he walked ahead of them, showing them the way to places where the grass was good and it was safe for his flock to graze. Whenever thieves tried to steal the sheep or wolves attacked them the shepherd never ran away like some bad shepherds did. He stayed with his sheep and fought off their attackers, even if he hurt himself

'I am just like the good shepherd,' Jesus explained. 'And the people who follow me are like those sheep – I look after them. I shall even give my life for them.'

The missing sheep

The second story was about a shepherd who had a hundred sheep to look after.

One evening when he counted them he found there were only ninety nine. A sheep was missing! What had happened to it? Had it been stolen? Had it wandered away and been eaten by a lion, or fallen over a cliff? The shepherd was very sad and very worried. He left the ninety nine sheep in the pasture and went into the hills to search for the missing one.

At last he found it, high on a crag in the mountains. The shepherd was delighted. He heaved the frightened animal on to his strong shoulders and carried it safely back to the flock. Then he called his friends together: 'Come on, everyone, I want to celebrate – I'm so happy that my lost sheep is safely back in the fold!'

This story had an extra, secret meaning, too. People who turn their backs on God and forget him are like the sheep which went missing. God is like the shepherd who searched for his one lost sheep and was glad when he found it, even though he still had ninety nine good sheep at home.

The flowers

Jesus wanted everyone to understand that God cares for people very much and is always ready to help those who trust him. Jesus knew his friends were often worried because they didn't have much money and they had left their jobs to follow him.

'Don't be anxious,' Jesus told them, pointing to the flowers which carpeted the grass by the sea of Galilee. 'Did you ever see a flower sit down to spin its beautiful clothes? Of course not! Yet see how brightly God dresses them! Even rich King Solomon in all his glorious robes never wore anything so splendid! If God takes so much trouble with the grass, won't he take even more care of you and give you clothes and food, too? So why don't you trust him? Expect God to look after you and stop worrying all the time!'

The wonderful harvest

Jesus' stories were always about familiar things like the flowers which everyone had seen. Everyone had seen shepherds working in the hills, too, and they all knew about farmers like the one in this next story.

Early one morning a farmer set out to sow his seed. He carried it in a big bag, and as he walked he scattered handfuls of seed over the ground. Some fell on the hard earth of the path and birds flew down at once and pecked it up. Some seed fell into stony ground where there was only a thin layer of soil. Green shoots sprang up very quickly, but they could not take root in the shallow earth — so as soon as the sun grew hot the young plants dried up and died.

Some of the seed fell among thorn bushes which choked the shoots so that they could not grow.

Some seed, however, fell into good soil where it grew and ripened until it stood thick and tall, ready for the harvest. The farmer was pleased, for the good ground gave back thirty, sixty, even a hundred times more corn than he had sown! It was a wonderful harvest!

After he had told the story, Jesus explained the secret meaning to his friends.

'The seed is our message about God's love. The hard earth path is like the hearts of some people who never accept what we tell them. The message soon disappears from their minds.

'Other people do understand and are thrilled by the message, but they don't want to do anything too hard. When trouble comes they give up easily and blame God. They are like the stony soil which only had a thin layer of good earth.

'Other people listen to our message, but all sorts of worries about money and the problems of everyday life spring up in their minds, like the thorns in the story, and choke the good news about God.

'But there *are* people who are so glad to hear about God's love that they start to lead lives that please him and they tell the good news to others, too. They are like the good soil that gives back more grain than the farmer sowed.'

The two houses

Jesus told another story about people who listened to his teaching.

'If you follow my teaching,' he said, 'you are like the wise man who wanted to build a house. He dug down through the sandy soil of the valley where he wanted to build it until he came to the rock. Then he built his house firmly, using the rock for a foundation. When the autumn rains came and flooded the valley, and storms shook the house it stood firmly.

'Another man built a house nearby, but he didn't bother to dig down to the rock, instead he built his house on the sand. When the autumn rains came the sandy soil was washed away. The house creaked and shook and came crashing down. The flood swept it away and there was nothing left of it.

'Those who don't follow my teaching are like that. When troubles come they can't stand firm.'

The two men

Jesus had another story about two very different men who went to pray in the temple. The first was a Pharisee, one of the Jewish leaders, and the second was a tax-collector.

The Pharisee thought he always kept God's laws. He swept proudly in through the temple doors and stood where everyone could see him. Loudly he told God how good he was: 'Thank you God, that I'm better than other people. I'm not a bit like that tax-man over there. I do everything that pleases you.'

The tax-man who had come in very quietly could only whisper with his head bent low, 'Have pity on me, God. I've done wrong and I'm sorry.'

Both men went home, but it was not the proud Pharisee who pleased God most. It was the tax-man who said, 'sorry'; and God forgave him.

parties because he was rich. Before long his money was spent, and his new friends disappeared, too. No one wanted him without money.

The lost son

In another story, Jesus taught how God is always longing to forgive anyone who owns up like the tax-man did.

A farmer had two sons. The elder was a stay-at-home, but the younger boy loved adventure.

'I want to see the world,' thought the younger son. 'When my father is dead, I'll get a share of his goods, but I want some money now. I'll go and ask my father for my share of his things. Then I'll leave home and do whatever I want.'

The farmer felt very sad that his son wanted to leave home because he loved the boy, but he let him do what he wanted. So, with a purse full of money, the younger son set off for a distant country.

At first he had plenty of fun and made a great many friends who were glad to invite him to their

He was all alone, and he didn't even have enough to buy food. He tried to find work, but the only job he could get was on a farm, looking after pigs.

He watched the pigs guzzling their food and he wished he could have something to eat, too. He would even have been glad to eat some of the pigs' bean pods. He began to think of his home where no one was ever hungry.

'My father is kind and treats everyone well, even the servants,' he thought. 'How stupid I am, sitting here starving! I'll go back home and tell my father I'm sorry. Perhaps he'll let me work for him as a servant if he doesn't want me back as a son!'

The more he thought about it, the better the idea seemed. Feeling happier than he had done for a very long time, the young man set off on his journey home.

Some time later, his father was looking out of the window, when he spotted a thin figure limping

along. The farmer stared. Then he saw that it was his younger son, and he raced down the road to meet him. He flung his arms round him and hugged and kissed him while the boy started to say, 'sorry'.

'Father, I've done wrong in God's eyes, and I've treated you badly, too,' he said. 'I'm not fit to be your son any more, but please take me back to be one of your hired servants.'

His father wouldn't hear of it. He hurried him into the house, calling to his servants, 'Bring the best robe and put it on my son! Give him a ring to wear and sandals, too. Kill the young calf! We'll have a splendid feast!'

The elder son was working for his father in the fields. When he came back to the house in the evening he heard the sound of music and dancing. The servants told him that his brother had come home. He stood in the doorway, sulking.

'Father never killed a calf for me to have a party,' he muttered,

'and I've stayed at the farm working while my brother was away enjoying himself. It's not fair!'

His father had to come out to persuade him to go in to the feast.

'You've always been with me,' he said, 'and everything I have now is yours. But it's right that we should be glad and celebrate today! I thought your brother was dead, but he's come to life again – he was lost, but now he's found!'

The good Samaritan

As well as teaching people about God and how to please him, Jesus wanted to show people how they should treat one another. Once one of the religious leaders asked Jesus a question. 'What must I do to go to heaven when I die?'

Jesus knew that the questioner was a clever man who was really trying to catch him out, so he asked another question in return.

'God gave us a law to tell us how to please him. What does it say?'

'We must love God with all our heart and love our neighbours just as much as we love ourselves,' answered the man.

'Then that is what you must do,' answered Jesus simply.

'Well, but who is my neighbour?' the clever man asked. And Jesus told a story to answer him.

The road from Jerusalem to Jericho goes through lonely country where there are plenty of rocks for robbers to hide behind. Nobody liked using the road, especially when they were on their own. One day a traveller set out from Jerusalem, and sure enough, before he had gone very far, a gang of thieves leapt out and attacked him. They snatched his bags, stripped off his cloak and beat him up. Then they ran off, leaving him badly hurt. He would certainly die if no one came by to help him.

As he lay there, he heard footsteps coming along the road. He was too weak to shout or move, but he felt sure that whoever it was would see him.

The passerby was a priest. He was going to Jerusalem to pray in the temple. He noticed the man, but he was too scared to stop in case the robbers attacked him, too.

Hastily he crossed over the road and walked by on the other side.

A little later another man came down the road. He was on his way to the temple, too. He looked at the wounded man for a moment, but then he crossed the road as well, and went on his way, leaving the man lying in the hot sun.

At last a Samaritan came by,

riding on a donkey. Jews and Samaritans hated one another, but this man felt sorry for the wounded Jew. He got off his donkey and searched in his bags for some cool oil and wine which he had with him. He used them to clean the man's cuts. Then he tore up his own clothes for bandages. He lifted the man on to his donkey and took him to an inn where he looked after him all night.

Next morning the Samaritan had to go on with his journey. He gave the innkeeper two silver coins.

'Look after him well,' he said. 'If you have to spend more money, I will repay you when I come back.'

'Who do you think really cared for the man who was robbed?' Jesus asked the clever man at the end of his story.

'The one who looked after him!' came the reply. The clever man didn't like admitting it was the Samaritan, one of the Jews' enemies!

But Jesus replied, 'Then you must go and behave in the same way.'

41

JESUS THE FRIEND

Keeping the Sabbath

Most people enjoyed listening to Jesus' stories and finding out more about God, but the priests were angry. They were afraid that Jesus was going to upset their laws.

One Saturday Jesus and his friends were walking through the cornfields. Saturday was the day which the Jews set aside to worship God. It was a special, holy day when no work could be done. The leaders had made up all sorts of rules about how the day should be spent.

Jesus and his friends felt hungry and they picked some ears of wheat as they walked along so that they could eat the nutty kernels. Some of the leaders came over to Jesus at once.

'Your friends are breaking the law! No one is allowed to work on the Sabbath! Picking ears of wheat is work!' they cried.

Jesus was angry. He knew that God wanted the Sabbath to be a happy day when people could worship him. The leaders had

invented so many rules that keeping them was a burden. Jesus tried to explain this to the leaders, but they were angry too and would not listen.

'Jesus keeps breaking our laws,' they muttered. They put their heads together and began to plot against Jesus.

One Saturday Jesus went into a synagogue to pray. There he saw a man with a crippled hand. The Jewish leaders watched closely. If Jesus healed the man it would count as work and he would have broken the law.

Jesus knew what they were thinking.

'When your sheep falls into a hole, you rescue it at once, even on the Sabbath,' he said.

Then he turned to the man.

'Stretch out your hand,' he ordered.

The man obeyed, and at once his hand was well and strong again.

The Jewish leaders were shocked and angry. They began to plot even harder to have Jesus killed.

Jesus helps a Roman soldier

The synagogue in Capernaum had been built for the Jewish people by a Roman officer. He was a good, just man who believed in God. He had a servant whom he treated well and liked very much. One day the servant grew ill. How worried his master was! He decided to ask Jesus for help.

'Yes, I'll come and make your servant well,' said Jesus.

'No,' replied the officer. 'I don't deserve to have you in my house, and you don't need to come. I know you are under God's authority, just as I am under my commander's. I give orders too, and my soldiers obey me at once. Just give the order and my servant will recover!'

Jesus was amazed.

'I have never met any of my people who believe like this foreigner!' he exclaimed. 'Go home. What you have believed will indeed happen.'

At that very moment the servant became well.

Jesus calms a storm

One evening Jesus and his friends wanted to find a quiet place away from the crowds so that they could rest and spend time together. They decided to take a fishing boat, and set off across the Sea of Galilee. Jesus was tired and he soon fell fast asleep. Suddenly a fierce wind blew up, making huge waves that crashed over the sides of the boat. Jesus' friends were terrified because they were fishermen and they knew how dangerous sudden storms could be. They woke Jesus at once. He stood up and looked around. He saw the tremendous waves, but he wasn't afraid.

'Be still!' he told the storm.

At once the wind dropped and the waves grew calm. His friends were amazed at his power.

'Who can this man really be?' they asked one another. 'Even the wind and sea obey him!'

Jesus feeds five thousand people

It was always difficult for Jesus and his friends to get away from the crowds to rest. People would even chase after a fishing boat if they caught sight of Jesus on board. As soon as he landed they gathered about him.

Once, when this happened, Jesus felt so sorry for the people that he stayed with them all day. When evening came everyone was hungry.

'Whatever will they find to eat?' asked Andrew, one of Jesus' friends. 'We'd better send them away to the villages to buy food.'

'Give them food yourselves!' said Jesus. 'How much bread do you have?'

'There's a boy here who has five loaves and two fishes,' replied Andrew, 'but they won't go very far in this crowd!'

Quietly Jesus took the basket the boy held out to him.

'Make the people sit down,' he told his friends.

Then he thanked God for the food. He broke the loaves into pieces and divided the fish. His friends began to share the food out among the people, and although there were five thousand in the crowd, there was more than enough for everybody. In fact, after they had finished eating, Jesus' friends filled twelve baskets with the bits that were left over.

Everyone was amazed at Jesus' power.

Some of the people wanted to make Jesus king, but he knew that was not what God wanted. He tried to make his friends understand that the work God had given him to do would be very different.

'My enemies will arrest me and kill me,' he warned them, 'but God will bring me back to life.'

Jesus helps ten sick men

Jesus and his friends were making their way through the countryside near Samaria. They had just arrived at a village when they saw ten men standing by themselves at a safe distance from everyone else. The men were ill with a terrible skin disease, and people were afraid that if they came too close they might catch it, too. The ten men begged Jesus to make them well, and he told them to go and show a priest that they were better. This was what the law said they had to do if they were cured. As soon as the men started off they became well again. Full of excitement, nine of the men rushed on their way to the priest, but one, who was a Samaritan, turned

back, praising God. He found Jesus and thanked him for making him well so that he no longer needed to hide away from everyone.

'There were ten of you, and you, the foreigner, are the only one who has come back to say thank you!' exclaimed Jesus. 'Go back home,' he told the happy man. 'Your faith has made you completely well again.'

Jesus and the children

Some families decided to bring their children to see Jesus. When they arrived, Jesus' friends tried to turn them away.

'Jesus is too busy to talk to children!' they said. Jesus heard this and he was angry.

'Don't send the children away!' he called. 'Let them come to me!'

The children crowded round him happily and Jesus put his arms round them. He turned to the grown-ups.

'You need to have faith like these children,' he told them. He touched the children and prayed that God would bless them.

Jesus and the rich young man

Jesus and his friends were saying goodbye to the children when a young man pushed eagerly through the crowd. Unlike many of the people who came to see Jesus, he looked well fed and well dressed. His beard was carefully cut and combed. He had rings on his fingers and jewels round his neck. Yet there was something the rich man needed. He wanted to go to heaven when he died.

'What must I do?' he asked Jesus.

'You must keep God's laws,' answered Jesus.

'I have obeyed them all my life, Teacher!'

Jesus looked very lovingly at the young man.

'There is still one thing. Sell everything you have. Give the money to the poor and follow me!'

Jesus spoke warmly, but the young man shook his head. He couldn't bring himself to give up his money. Sadly he walked away.

Jesus and the little tax-collector

However, there was another rich man who wanted to meet Jesus. He was the chief tax-collector of Jericho and his name was Zacchaeus. One day Zacchaeus heard that Jesus was coming to Jericho. At once he rushed down the road to join the crowd who were waiting for Jesus.

Zacchaeus was short and dumpy. He couldn't see over the other people, and he knew that no one would make way for him because he was a tax-collector and a cheat. He charged everyone too much and kept the extra money for himself.

Suddenly he spotted a big tree growing beside the road. Hoping that no one was looking, he clambered up into the branches. Now he had a splendid view of Jesus when he passed underneath!

Zacchaeus had heard that Jesus made friends with tax-collectors, but he couldn't believe it when Jesus looked up into the tree and called his name.

'Come down, Zacchaeus! I must stay at your home today!'

Joyfully, Zacchaeus scrambled down the tree, never minding who saw.

He gave Jesus a splendid welcome, but the crowd followed him to his house grumbling, 'What's Jesus doing, mixing with someone like Zacchaeus?'

Suddenly their grumbles changed to loud cheering. Zacchaeus had started giving his things away.

'Come on, everyone!' he shouted. 'Help yourselves! Have I cheated anyone here? Take this then. Take four times as much!'

When he went back inside, his house seemed bare, but Jesus was there, smiling and pleased.

'Well done,' he said to Zacchaeus, and Zacchaeus felt very happy. He knew that he belonged to God now, and that God had forgiven him all the wrong he had done.

Jesus and the blind beggar

A blind beggar called Bartimaeus lived in Jericho, too. He was sitting by the roadside as usual, asking the passersby for money when he heard a huge crowd come tramping along. Their feet scuffed up the dust and sent it swirling round the blind man.

'What's happening?' he called out.

'Jesus is coming,' cried the crowd.

At once blind Bartimaeus began to shout, 'Help me, Jesus! Help me!'

Unkind people in the crowd told him to be quiet, but Bartimaeus went on yelling. Then someone said, 'Get up! Jesus heard you shouting. He wants you to come to him.'

Bartimaeus jumped up. He tottered forward to Jesus, his knobbly fingers stretched out in front of him to guide him along.

'What do you want me to do for you?' asked Jesus.

'Oh, Teacher, I want to see!' gasped Bartimaeus, breathlessly.

'Then see!' said Jesus. 'Your faith has made you well.'

The blind man blinked. He looked up, and the first thing he saw was the face of Jesus. Joyfully he followed him along the road, gazing round him at everything and shouting loud praises to God.

Jesus and the two sisters

Jesus had two special friends who often invited him to stay with them. They were two sisters called Martha and Mary. One day, when Jesus was visiting them, Martha was very busy cleaning and cooking, but Mary sat down beside Jesus and listened to him.

Poor Martha felt very upset.

'Make my sister come and help me with the work!' she said to Jesus.

But he replied, 'Martha, Martha, you are worried and anxious about your work in the kitchen, but Mary has her work to do as well, learning about God, and that is best!'

Jesus raises Lazarus

Martha and Mary had a brother called Lazarus. One day Lazarus became seriously ill, and within two days he was dead. Jesus was far away at the time, but the two sisters sent someone to him with the news.

By the time Jesus arrived at Bethany where the family lived, Lazarus had been buried. Martha came out to meet Jesus.

'If you had been here, my brother would not have died,' she said, 'but I know that God will do whatever you ask him.'

'Martha,' said Jesus, 'everyone who believes in me will rise again from death. Do you believe this?'

'Yes,' she answered him firmly. 'Yes, I believe what you say; you are the Son of God.'

Then Mary came out to Jesus. She too was sure that he could have healed her brother. She was crying bitterly, and so were Lazarus' friends who came with her. Jesus felt very sad. As he walked with them to the place

where Lazarus was buried he began to cry, too.

The body had been wrapped in linen cloths and laid in a cave which had been closed up with a huge, round stone. Jesus told them to remove the stone. Then he prayed to God and called loudly, 'Lazarus, come out!'

At once, Lazarus appeared at the entrance of the cave, alive, but still wrapped in linen cloths.

'Unwind these cloths and let him go,' said Jesus.

Now many more people believed in him, but the priests were furious. They wanted more than ever to have Jesus killed, and they watched him carefully, waiting for a chance to seize him.

THE EASTER STORY

Jesus goes to Jerusalem

Jesus knew very well that his life was in danger, but he knew, too, that it was God's plan for him to die and come to life again. So he set off firmly for Jerusalem, to celebrate the Passover Festival there, even though the city would be full of his enemies.

As they made their way towards the city, Jesus had a surprise for two of his friends.

'You remember our holy writings say that the king whom God is sending will ride into Jerusalem on a donkey? You'll find a donkey in the next village. Untie him and bring him to me. If anyone asks, say, "the Master needs him," and they will let you take him.'

Full of excitement the two friends ran off.

They found the donkey easily, and started to untie his rope.

'Hey! Stop!' a man shouted from a doorway. 'What are you doing, taking that donkey?'

'The Master needs him!' said the friends, as Jesus had told them.

'Oh, well, that's different!' said the man. 'Treat him carefully, won't you? No one has ever ridden him before, but if Jesus wants him, he can have him.'

They untied the donkey and led him to Jesus.

Crowds of people were flocking to Jerusalem for the Passover Festival. Everybody was happy because of the holiday, and when they saw Jesus they cheered with excitement. 'Here comes the king!' they shouted.

They cut down palm branches from the trees and waved them in the air. Some people even spread their cloaks in the road, and the donkey walked over them as he carried Jesus slowly into the city. On through the narrow streets they went, to the beautiful temple where Jews from all over the world gathered to praise God.

Jesus clears the temple

At once Jesus saw something that made him very angry.

The temple courtyard was like a market place, where people could buy birds and animals to offer to God. Lambs bleated loudly, and white doves cooed in cages.

Special coins had to be used inside the temple area, so every-one had to change their money, just as though they were going to a foreign country. The money changers were cheats and kept most of the change. So Jesus seized hold of a whip and drove them out.

He toppled over their tables. Coins rolled in all directions. Then the temple was in an uproar! Doves flew free. Sheep butted one another and calves mooed, while the dealers yelled and raged.

'God wants his temple to be a quiet place where people can pray to him!' cried Jesus. 'You dealers are wrong! You have made God's temple like a robber's den! Get out!'

The priests and leaders, who hated Jesus, were furious with him. It was their job to keep order in the temple. So they tried to trap him with a trick question.

'Teacher,' they said politely, 'should we pay taxes to the Romans or not?'

If Jesus said, 'no', he would be in trouble with the Romans. If he said 'yes', the people would be angry, for the Jews hated having to pay taxes and obey the Roman law. His friends waited anxiously to see what he would do.

'Let me see a coin,' he said. 'Whose name and head are stamped on it?'

'The Roman Emperor's,' they replied.

'Then pay the Roman Emperor what is his, and pay God what belongs to him,' answered Jesus.

Silenced, they slunk away, but Jesus knew that they still watched him closely.

Jesus and the expensive perfume

Every day for the next week Jesus taught the crowds in the temple, but at night, for safety, he and his friends left Jerusalem to stay in a little village close by. One evening a woman called Mary Magdalene came to find Jesus. She brought a jar of expensive perfume and she loved Jesus so much that she poured the whole jar over his

Jesus and the poor widow

As they walked about the temple, Jesus and his friends saw rich people dropping silver coins into the collecting boxes. Then they noticed a poor woman. She was a widow with no family to help her, and it was plain that she never had enough to eat. She dropped two small copper coins into the box.

'Look, friends,' said Jesus, 'this poor woman has put in far more than all the rich people we have seen.'

'Has she?' his friends asked, amazed.

'Yes,' Jesus answered. 'You see they gave God only what they thought they could spare. They have plenty of money left, but she is so poor she had only those two coins. She has given God all the money she had.'

head and feet. A wonderful scent filled the room. Mary's tears fell on Jesus' feet as she kissed them and wiped them with her hair.

'What a waste!' said Judas, one of Jesus' followers. 'Mary could have sold this perfume and given the money to the poor.'

'No,' replied Jesus. 'Mary has done a beautiful thing for me before I die.'

Jesus and Judas

Mary was glad, but Judas scowled angrily at Jesus' words. He looked after the money for Jesus and the others and he used to help himself from their supply. If Mary had sold her perfume there would have been more for him to steal. Now, every day, he grew greedier for money and he began to be angry with Jesus because he cared for different things. At last he went to the priests.

'What will you give me if I help you to capture Jesus?' he asked.

They counted thirty silver coins into his hand. Judas slipped away, but he was watchful now, waiting for a time when Jesus was alone and his enemies could capture him without any trouble.

The Passover meal

Towards the end of the week the time came for the Passover which the Jews celebrated with a special supper of flat bread and lamb with sauce and herbs. Jesus found a secret room in Jerusalem where he could eat the Passover meal in safety with his friends. As they sat at the table Jesus stood up and took off his long tunic. He tied a towel round his waist, poured water into a bowl, and went round his friends in turn, washing the dust of the city streets from their feet.

Simon Peter said, 'Lord, you mustn't wash my feet like a servant!'

'I'm washing your feet because I love you, Peter,' said Jesus. 'My friends, I am happy to work for you like a servant. You must be ready, too, to serve one another in humble ways.'

Jesus sat down again. 'One of you is going to hand me over to my enemies,' he said sadly.

'Who could it be?' they wondered anxiously, but Judas knew. Quietly he slipped outside. Then Jesus took some bread, broke it and shared it with his friends.

'This is my body, which is given for you,' he said. 'When you break and eat bread together like this, you must remember me.'

Sad and puzzled, they shared the bread.

Then Jesus passed the cup of wine round among them.

'Drink this, all of you,' he said. 'This is my blood, which will be poured out so that everyone's sins can be forgiven by God.'

Judas betrays Jesus

They did not understand. Why did he keep talking about dying when every day crowds followed him and praised him? Sadly they left the room and went with him to a quiet garden outside the city where Jesus liked to pray.

On the way Jesus warned them yet again of all that was to happen.

'I'll stick by you,' declared Simon Peter. 'Even if all the others run away and leave you.'

'Before you hear the cock crow tomorrow morning you will say three times that you do not know me,' said Jesus. 'Wait here, all of you,' he added. 'Don't go to sleep. Stay awake and pray for me.'

Then he went further into the garden and prayed alone: 'Father, if it is possible, don't let me die this horrible death!'

His hair stuck to his forehead, wet with sweat. With a great effort he cried out, 'Father, don't do what I want. Do what you know is best.'

He returned to his friends and

68

found them asleep.

'Could you not stay awake?' asked Jesus. 'Get up now. Here come my enemies.'

Into the quiet garden came Judas, followed by the temple police and a rough crowd, armed with sticks and spears. The chief priests had sent them all to capture Jesus.

'The man I kiss is the one you want,' muttered Judas to the police.

He went straight to Jesus. 'Peace, Teacher,' Judas said, and kissed him.

Jesus looked steadily at Judas. 'Why are you here, friend?' he asked gently. 'Have you come to give me away with your kiss?'

Jesus is arrested

Then the soldiers grabbed Jesus and held him securely.

'Don't hurt my friends,' Jesus warned them.

Simon Peter had a sword hidden under his cloak. He wanted to defend Jesus, and he struck at a slave and cut off the man's ear.

'Put your sword away, Simon,' said Jesus. 'I shall go with them willingly, for this is the way my Father has chosen for me.'

The crowd fell silent.

'Did you have to come with sticks and spears to capture me?'

Jesus asked them. 'Day after day I went to the temple. You all saw me there, but none of you arrested me then.'

He knew that they had been afraid to arrest him because of the crowds. He touched the wounded man and healed his ear.

'Now is the time for the powers of darkness to have their way,' Jesus said.

The soldiers hurried him roughly out of the garden. His terrified friends scattered among the trees, leaving Jesus alone in the power of the men who hated him and wanted to kill him.

Now that they had managed to capture Jesus at last, his enemies had to find a reason to have him killed. All night long they asked him questions. The leaders brought in people who told lies about Jesus but none of their stories agreed.

Finally, at dawn, the high priest asked, 'Are you the Son of God?'

'Yes, I am,' Jesus replied.

'He claims to be God! That's against our holy law!' cried the high priest.

'He's guilty!' the others agreed. 'He must die!'

Peter lets Jesus down

Outside, in the courtyard, there was a fire where the soldiers and the leaders' servants could warm themselves while they waited.

Simon Peter had slipped in with the crowd that came with Jesus, and he went and stood by the fire.

The high priest's servants noticed him.

'Weren't you one of Jesus' friends?' asked a girl.

'Oh, no, I don't even know him,' declared Simon Peter uneasily, but a little later one of the men spotted the strong fisherman.

'Hey, this fellow's one of them, too!' he said.

'Me? Certainly not!' lied Simon Peter.

'Come on, you can't fool us! You're from Galilee, too. Your accent gives you away. Of course you were with Jesus.'

'No, I don't know him!' Simon Peter shouted.

Beyond the courtyard the first pale streaks of daylight showed in the sky. A cock close by crowed loudly. Then Simon Peter remembered what Jesus had told him – that before the cock crowed in the morning he would say three times that he did not know Jesus.

Peter rushed outside and cried bitterly.

Jesus and the Roman governor

The Jewish leaders were not allowed to put people to death. Only the Roman rulers could do that. So Jesus was sent to the Roman governor, a man called Pontius Pilate.

'We've brought you a real trouble-maker,' the priests warned Pilate. 'He stirs up our people against the Romans. He even calls himself a king!''

Pilate looked at Jesus curiously. 'Are you a king?' he asked.

'So you say,' answered Jesus, and he would not reply to any more of Pilate's questions.

Pilate looked helplessly at his prisoner. He knew that Jesus had done nothing that deserved death, but he knew that the priests wanted him killed. Pilate did not want to annoy the priests. He had an idea.

He led Jesus outside and showed him to the crowd which was waiting there.

'You know I always free one of your prisoners at Passover time,' Pilate told the crowd. 'Here is Jesus. Shall I let him go?'

'No!' shouted the people. Then someone yelled, 'Free Barabbas instead!' and other voices joined in, although Barabbas was a bandit.

Pilate was afraid of the angry crowd, so he had Barabbas set free and handed Jesus over to the Roman soldiers, who beat him cruelly. They made a crown from thorny twigs and forced it on to Jesus' head. Then they wrapped a purple cloak round him and bowed to him, jeering, 'Long live the king!'

At last Pilate took Jesus out to the crowd again. 'Here is your king,' he said. 'What do you want me to do with him? He has done nothing to deserve death.'

But the priests had persuaded the people that Jesus ought to die, and the crowd yelled, 'The cross! Let him die on the cross!'

It was the same crowd who had welcomed him to the city only five days before.

Jesus is crucified

So Jesus was led away to die. He had to carry his own cross, but his shoulders were torn and bleeding from the soldiers' whips, and he stumbled and fell under the weight. So the soldiers seized a man called Simon, who had come from Cyrene in North Africa to keep the festival in Jerusalem, and forced him to carry Jesus' heavy load. Simon remembered that cross for the rest of his life.

Beyond the city walls was a place called 'Skull Hill'. There they laid Jesus down on the cross and hammered nails through his hands and feet.

Jesus said, 'Father, forgive them. They don't understand what they are doing.'

Two robbers were nailed to crosses on either side of him.

Some of the soldiers played dice to pass the time. The winner would have for his prize the clothes which Jesus had worn. A large crowd watched Jesus, and their leaders jeered, 'Get yourself off the cross, king!'

One of the robbers joined in, but the other said, 'We are both getting what we deserve, but this man hasn't done anything wrong!' Turning his head towards Jesus he said, 'Remember me when you come back as king.'

'Today you shall be in Paradise with me,' Jesus answered firmly.

It was nine o'clock when they nailed Jesus to the cross. At midday the sky grew black. Jesus called out into the darkness, 'My God, my God, why have you deserted me?'

Some people heard him and wondered if, even now, God would rescue him, but nothing happened.

Jesus had only a little strength left. 'I'm so thirsty!' he gasped.

Soldiers soaked a sponge with sour wine and lifted it up to moisten his lips.

'Everything is finished,' Jesus cried. He bowed his head and died.

Jesus is alive

Two of his secret followers begged Pilate for Jesus' body. They wrapped it in strips of linen cloth and took it to a garden where there was a new grave cut in the rock. Some of the women who had been Jesus' friends too, followed the men to the garden. They watched while the men rolled a heavy stone in front of the entrance to the grave, and they all went home very sadly. The holy

Magdalene made her way to the garden. With a shock she saw that the grave stood wide open. She ran to fetch Simon Peter and another friend, John.

The two men raced to the grave. It was quite empty. There was no body at all. Only the linen cloths lay on the ground. Puzzled, the men went away, but Mary stayed by the grave, crying. She did not see a man standing close by.

'What is the matter? Why are you crying?' the man asked her. She thought he must be the gardener.

'Sir,' she said, 'they've moved his body. Do you know where it's been taken?'

'Mary!' said the man, and suddenly she recognised him. It was Jesus!

'Master!' she exclaimed happily, drying her tears.

'Go and tell my friends I am alive,' said Jesus joyfully.

Mary ran back at once to Jesus' ·friends, but they wouldn't believe her.

'Alive? It can't be true!' they muttered.

Sabbath was just beginning, so they could do no work, but as soon as Saturday evening came, the women began preparing perfumes and spices to lay in the linen grave cloths. It was the only way they could show how much they cared for Jesus.

Early on Sunday morning Mary

A walk to Emmaus

That afternoon two of the men left Jerusalem for a nearby village called Emmaus. As they walked together along the road, talking to each other, a stranger caught up with them.

'What are you discussing?' he asked.

'Haven't you heard about Jesus of Nazareth?' they said. 'We thought he was the one sent by God to help us, but he has been put to death. Now some women are saying he is alive again. Certainly his body has disappeared. It's very puzzling.'

'But don't our holy writings say that God's promised king must die and rise again?' asked the stranger, and he explained many things to them as they walked along.

When they arrived at Emmaus it was getting dark and they asked him to stay with them. So he went to their house and shared their

supper. He took the bread, thanked God and broke it, just as Jesus used to do. Then they saw he *was* Jesus. They were overjoyed, but he disappeared immediately.

The two men rushed straight back to Jerusalem. They wanted to tell the others, but their friends had their own exciting news to tell. 'Jesus is alive! Simon Peter saw him, too!'

'We know he's alive. He met us on the road and talked to us!' the two men answered.

Jesus meets his friends

Suddenly Jesus was in the room with them. They were terrified for they thought he must be a ghost. Quickly Jesus spoke to them.

'I'm no ghost. Touch me. You can't touch a ghost!'

Still they could hardly believe it. Yet there he was, showing them the marks in his hands and feet where he had been nailed to the cross.

'Have you any food, friends?' he asked.

They gave him some fish, and watched, amazed, as he ate.

'Soon you must go and tell everyone that I died and came alive again so that their sins could be forgiven,' Jesus told them. 'But you must wait here in Jerusalem until God sends the Holy Spirit to be with you in my place. He will give you the help you need.'

Jesus and Thomas

One of Jesus' friends, Thomas, was out when Jesus met the others. He didn't believe their news.

'Unless I actually touch the scars in his hands, I won't believe Jesus is alive!' Thomas said.

Eight days later Thomas was with the others and Jesus came again.

'Look, Thomas,' he said, 'here are the marks of the nails. Touch these scars and believe.'

Thomas fell to his knees. 'You are my Lord and my God!' he declared.

'Thomas, you believe because you can see me,' said Jesus, 'but how happy people will be who believe in me without seeing me!'

Jesus and Peter

Later on, some of Jesus' friends went home to Galilee, back to their fishing. One night they went out in their boat, but they didn't catch a single fish. At daybreak someone on the shore shouted to them, 'Throw out your net to the right!'

They tossed the net out, and at once it was weighed down with fish.

'That's Jesus!' John said to Simon Peter.

Simon leapt into the sea and swam to Jesus. On the beach Jesus had a fire blazing and some fish ready cooked.

'Bring some more fish,' he said. Simon Peter went back and hauled the heavy net ashore.

'Breakfast's ready!' Jesus called.

After breakfast Jesus asked Simon Peter quietly, three times, 'Simon, do you love me?'

'Yes, Lord,' answered Simon

Peter each time, remembering sadly how he had lied three times about Jesus.

'Then look after my followers,' said Jesus. Now Simon Peter knew that Jesus still trusted him.

Jesus goes back to Heaven

Soon the time came for Jesus to leave his friends and go back to heaven to be with God. One day he and his close friends went out of the city. They climbed a hill. Jesus prayed that his friends would always know God's love and peace, and he gave them a

command: 'You must tell everyone the good news,' Jesus said. 'Remember, I am alive for ever and I shall be with you always, right to the end of time, just as I told you.'

Then he disappeared from their sight. They would not see him again on earth, but they knew the Holy Spirit would come and help them.

They went back to Jerusalem and they started going to the temple every day to thank God for Jesus. They knew that God had sent him to die and come to life again so that everyone who believed in him could be freed from the power of wrong-doing, death and evil.

'Jesus is alive!' they sang, knowing that from then on the whole world would be different.

THE FIRST CHRISTIANS

The new helper

One morning, six weeks later, Jesus' friends met together to pray as usual. Suddenly the roar of a rushing wind filled the room where they were sitting. Leaping flames touched their heads, and they felt that God was very close to them. The special helper, God's Holy Spirit, had come, just as Jesus had promised. They began to praise God excitedly and at once they found themselves speaking in different languages, which God's Holy Spirit made them able to do. Still praising God, they ran out into the street.

The sound of their laughter and happy shouts soon drew a crowd round them. People from many foreign countries had come to Jerusalem for the Jewish festival of Pentecost. They were amazed to hear Jesus' friends talking about God in their own languages. Some people tried to turn it into a joke.

'These men are drunk!' they jeered. 'That's why they're shouting and talking like this!'

'No!' Peter declared firmly. 'We're not drunk, how could we be? It's far too early in the morning! God has sent us his Spirit and now we can tell you about Jesus. Jesus is God's Son and you put him to death here in Jerusalem. But God has brought him back to life, just as he promised in our holy writings.'

When the people heard what Peter said they were frightened and sorry. 'What must we do?' they asked.

'If you believe in Jesus you must stop doing wrong,' replied Peter. 'Then be baptised in his name, and God will forgive you. He will give you his Holy Spirit to help you to do things that please him.'

'We must do what Peter says,' many agreed. About three thousand people decided to be baptised that day. They too were strengthened by the power of the Holy Spirit and they listened eagerly as Peter and the others taught them more about Jesus.

Because they knew that God had forgiven them, and given them the Holy Spirit to help them to please him, the new followers of Jesus felt very happy. They all shared everything they had. They met in one another's houses to eat their meals and pray together. Every day they went to the temple to praise God, and they were so full of joy that more and more people kept joining them.

Peter and John heal a lame man

One day Peter and his friend John were going into the temple when they met a lame beggar. He used to sit beside one of the temple gates all day, calling, 'Give me some money! I've never walked in all my life. Give me a coin so that I can buy food!'

Peter and John stopped, and the beggar watched them hopefully.

'I have no money to give you,' Peter said, 'but I shall give you what I have. In the name of Jesus I command you: get up and walk!'

He helped the beggar to stand. At once the man felt strength flow into his weak feet and ankles. He let go of Peter's hand and started to walk. Soon he was jumping and leaping into the air shouting, 'Look, I can walk! I can really move about! How good God is! Thank you, God! You've made me able to walk like everyone else after I'd been lame all my life.'

He ran into the temple where everyone who knew him was amazed to see him walking about, praising God.

Peter and John in trouble

Peter explained to the people in the temple that it was the power of Jesus that had made the lame man walk again. Some of the priests overheard and were furious. They thought they had got rid of Jesus! They actually had Peter and John arrested and kept in prison overnight. In spite of this, many of the people who saw what happened to the lame man became followers of Jesus, too.

Next day all the Jewish leaders, including the high priest, met together and questioned Peter and John.

'Where did you get the power to make a lame man walk?' the high priest demanded.

'We healed the man in the name of Jesus,' Peter explained. Then the Holy Spirit helped him to add bravely, 'You ordered Jesus to be put to death, but God brought him back to life, and now Jesus is the only one who can save us and help us!'

The leaders listened in amazement.
'What shall we do?' they said to one another.
'We can't punish men who healed a lame man! It's the talk of Jerusalem already! But we must stop this new faith before more people stop worshipping God in our way and

start following Jesus.'

So they told the two friends never to use the name of Jesus again.

'You are our leaders,' Peter and John replied, 'but God comes first, and we must do what he wants — we just can't stop telling everyone about Jesus!'

The leaders could say no more. They had to let Peter and John go.

Quickly the two made their way back to their friends. Together they all prayed that God would make them brave enough to go on talking about Jesus, no matter what the rulers threatened to do.

More trouble

God answered their prayers, and more and more people believed in Jesus. Crowds flocked in from the country, bringing sick friends with them and they were all made well.

The high priest and his followers were so angry that they had Peter and John arrested again and locked up in prison. That night

God sent an angel to their cell.

'Go back to the temple. Stand where everyone can see you, and tell them about Jesus,' said the angel, unlocking the barred gates.

Peter and John obeyed at once. When the high priest got up next morning and sent his men to the prison no one could find the prisoners! While they were wondering what could have happened and checking all the locks, a man rushed in: 'Those men you locked up last night are standing in the temple this very minute teaching everyone about Jesus,' he said breathlessly.

The high priest sent for them at once.

'We ordered you not to teach about Jesus,' the high priest thundered, but Peter answered boldly, 'We must do what God wants. He brought Jesus back to life, and we must tell people what he has done!'

When the priests heard this, they wanted to put Peter and his friends to death, but one of the leaders, a wise teacher called Gamaliel, whom everyone respected, advised them to be careful.

'If this new faith is just a made-up story, it will soon fade away and be forgotten. But if it is from God nothing you can do will stop it. Be careful! You might find yourselves fighting against God!'

So the priests had Peter and John beaten and then let them go. The friends were glad that God had let them suffer because they believed in Jesus. They took no notice of the priests but kept on telling everyone their good news.

Stephen

The new group of Jesus' followers soon had some other problems to face. Although they were all Jewish, they came from different countries and some spoke Jewish languages while others spoke only Greek. Some families were rich, but most were very poor. Every day they shared out their food, but the Greek-speaking families began to complain that they weren't getting enough. At last Peter and his ten friends, who had been the first followers of Jesus, called the whole group together.

'Choose seven men whom you know are wise and full of God's Holy Spirit, and put them in

charge of the money and the food supplies. Then everyone will get all they need,' they said.

One of the men who was chosen was called Stephen. He loved Jesus so much that he was able to do many wonderful things for the sick and needy people. He spoke so bravely about Jesus that the priests and leaders noticed and became his enemies.

Young Jewish men used to go to Jerusalem to learn more about the law from the priests. One young student called Saul heard about the followers of Jesus. Like the priests, he decided that they were wrong and ought to be stopped. One day Saul heard Stephen teaching in a synagogue, telling everyone that Jesus was alive.

'Jesus is with God now,' Stephen declared, 'but he is still helping us to lead lives which please God.'

Saul stared angrily at Stephen. 'This man must be stopped!' he hissed to a friend who was with him. 'Stephen and the others who follow Jesus are spoiling the way we Jews have tried to worship and please God for hundreds of years!'

Saul's friend nodded. Other Jewish leaders agreed with Saul. They made a plot to arrest Stephen. Soon he was on trial for his life.

Stephen faced his judges fearlessly. 'We can read in our holy writings that God sent to our people teachers to show us how to please him. Now in our time he has sent us his own Son, Jesus, but you still wouldn't listen. Instead you killed him!'

'And we'll kill you, too!' they snarled, but Stephen looked up and his eyes shone.

'I see Jesus in heaven with God, sharing his power!' he cried.

At this, they dragged him out of the city. They tossed their cloaks to Saul so that their arms were free to pick up heavy stones and hurl them at Stephen. Badly wounded, Stephen managed to pray, 'Lord Jesus, take me to you. Don't blame them for this, Lord!'

Saul listened angrily. He was glad to see Stephen die.

It was no longer safe to be a follower of Jesus. Saul and his friends wanted to destroy the new faith completely. Believers were dragged off to prison and punished. Many of them were forced to leave Jerusalem, but wherever they went they told people about Jesus, and the new faith spread all over the country.

Philip in Samaria

One man, called Philip, went to Samaria telling everyone there about Jesus. They were all amazed when they saw lame people walk and evil spirits driven away through the power of Jesus.

Philip baptised all the people who wanted to follow Jesus. There were so many new believers that Peter and John came over from Jerusalem to meet them. They prayed for the new believers to receive the Holy Spirit, too, so that they could have his power to help them to serve God.

The Ethiopian treasurer

At about this time, a very important man was on his way home from Jerusalem. He was the Queen of Ethiopia's treasurer. He loved God and wanted to learn more about him. As he rode home in his chariot he was reading from the Bible. God guided Philip to him, and he ran up to the treasurer's chariot. When Philip saw that the man was reading the Bible, he asked him if he understood it.

'How can I, without someone to help me?' replied the Ethiopian. He invited Philip to get into the chariot with him and explain the chapter he was reading. Philip agreed, and as he explained the chapter he told the treasurer about Jesus.

After a little while they drove past a pool of water. 'I believe everything you have told me,' said the treasurer, 'and look! There's some water! Can't you baptise me now, so that I can be a follower of Jesus, too?'

They got out of the chariot and Philip baptised him. Then the treasurer drove home happily, eager to tell his friends in Ethiopia about his new faith.

Saul meets Jesus

Meanwhile, Saul went on attacking everyone in Jerusalem who followed Jesus. He realised that the new faith was growing in other towns too, so he asked the high priest to let him go to the city of Damascus to arrest the believers there as well.

'I'll drag them back here in chains!' shouted Saul.

The high priest gave him permission, and Saul set out for Damascus. Suddenly, as he was riding along, a dazzling light shone in his eyes. Blinded, he fell to the ground. Then he heard a voice speaking to him: 'Saul, Saul, why are you attacking me?'

'Who are you, Lord?' Saul asked, amazed.

'I am Jesus,' came the answer. 'When you attack my followers you attack me, too. Get up now and go into Damascus. You will be told what to do there.'

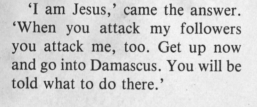

The men who were travelling with Saul heard the voice, but could see no one. They watched as Saul stood up uncertainly. He was completely blind and they had to lead him into Damascus.

For three days he stayed in a house there without eating or drinking anything, spending the whole time in prayer. Meanwhile, the Lord Jesus was preparing someone to help him. A man called Ananias saw Jesus in a dream.

'Go and help Saul,' said Jesus. 'He is staying in Straight Street.'

'Oh no, Lord, I've heard about that man,' answered Ananias. 'He's our worst enemy!'

'Go and help him,' Jesus repeated. 'I have chosen him to tell people all over the world about me.'

So Ananias went to Saul and laid his hands on his head. 'Brother, Saul, the Lord Jesus sent me to you. He wants you to see again.'

At once something like fish scales fell from Saul's eyes and he could see. He asked to be baptised straightaway as a sign that he followed Jesus. Only then did he have something to eat.

Saul escapes from Damascus

Saul stayed in Damascus and visited all the synagogues in the city. He told everyone what had happened to him.

'I know now that Jesus is the Son of God,' he said.

Many people who heard him came to believe, too, but others refused to follow Jesus. 'Saul's deserted us and joined those mistaken followers of Jesus,' they said. 'We must kill him before he spreads his story further. Let's keep a watch on all the city gates. He won't be able to sneak out of Damascus now!'

But Saul's new friends made plans, too. One night when it was dark, they hid Saul in a basket and lowered it over the city wall. So Saul escaped and hurried back to Jerusalem to join the other believers there. He hoped it would not be too hard for them to trust him.

At first they *were* afraid to trust Saul, but there was one man, called Barnabas, who did believe his story. He took Saul to the leaders of the group and told them what had happened to him.

'Saul has already risked his life for the Lord Jesus,' Barnabas explained warmly. So at last the believers welcomed Saul. He talked to everyone about Jesus, especially to the men who had planned Stephen's death. They were angry and tried to kill him, too, so his new friends sent him back to his family's home in the large seaport of Tarsus where he would be safe.

The churches grow

Now there was a time of peace for the followers of Jesus. Arrests and punishments hadn't stopped their faith and in the peaceful time it went on growing. They knew that Jesus was with them, no matter where they went. When they made new friends they told them about Jesus, and soon there were groups of people far and wide

who followed Jesus and loved God. They cared for one another and shared their belongings, just like the first believers in Jerusalem. These groups were called 'churches'. More and more people joined them.

Peter had a busy time now. He left Jerusalem and travelled through all the towns round about. In the town of Lydda he healed a man who had lain in bed, quite unable to move, for eight whole years. After that many more people came to believe in Jesus.

Dorcas

Near Lydda, in the port of Joppa, there lived a woman called Dorcas, who liked to help poor people because she loved Jesus. One day she grew very ill, and soon she died. When her friends heard, they asked Peter to come to Joppa.

As soon as he arrived, a sad crowd of women showed him the clothes that Dorcas had sewn for them. Peter went up to the room where Dorcas' body lay. He knelt by her bed and prayed. Then he said to the dead woman, 'Dorcas, get up!'

At once Dorcas opened her eyes and sat up. Peter helped her to her feet and called her friends.

The wonderful news spread all over Joppa and many people believed in Jesus. Everybody wanted Peter to tell them more about Jesus, so he agreed to stay on in Joppa.

Peter's dream

Houses in that part of the world had flat roofs where people could store their belongings, and which they could use as an extra room in hot weather. One day Peter went up on the roof of the house where he was staying in Joppa to pray. While he was there, God gave him a special dream. Peter saw a big sheet coming down from the sky, full of animals. A voice told him to kill an animal for his dinner. At first Peter was pleased because he was hungry, but then he saw that the animals were all of the kind that Jews are forbidden to eat by their law.

'No, Lord,' he said. 'I can't eat that!'

But God told him that everything he had made was good, and again invited him to eat.

At last Peter woke up. He was wondering what his dream meant when some men called to see him. They had been sent by a Roman officer called Cornelius, who wanted Peter to come to his house and tell him about Jesus. Jews were not allowed to mix with foreigners – but Peter remembered his dream. Now he understood that in God's eyes there were no differences between Jews and foreigners. God made them all, just as he made different sorts of animals for food. So Peter went with the men to meet the Roman officer.

Peter and Cornelius

Cornelius was delighted to see Peter. Although he was a Roman, he loved and worshipped God. He led Peter into his house where his friends and relations were waiting, too, to hear about God and his son Jesus.

'God has shown me that he loves everyone, no matter what race they belong to,' said Peter. He started to tell them about Jesus.

While he was speaking the power of God filled the room and the Holy Spirit came to Cornelius and his friends. They found themselves praising God in other languages, just as Jesus' friends had done in Jerusalem. The Jewish believers from Joppa who had gone with Peter were amazed, but Peter baptised Cornelius and his friends in the name of Jesus.

Peter in prison

Soon the peaceful time came to an end and trouble started again for the followers of Jesus. In Jerusalem life grew very dangerous, for King Herod Agrippa himself began to help the priests to hunt out the friends of Jesus. Fisherman James, who had left his boat years before to follow Jesus, was killed, and Peter, back from Joppa, was arrested. He was closely guarded by four soldiers.

The followers of Jesus met together to pray for him, and they had a special meeting on the evening before his trial.

That same night Peter was sleeping, chained between two guards. More soldiers guarded the gates. Suddenly a great light shone in his cell. An angel shook Peter awake.

'Get up at once!'

The heavy chains fell from Peter's wrists. He was free! Not sure whether he really was awake or still only dreaming, Peter followed the angel past the sleeping guards. The prison gate opened wide for them and they walked out. Peter found himself alone in the empty street. The cold air convinced him that this was no dream. God had freed him! He ran to find his friends.

Hurriedly he knocked at the door of the house where his friends were still praying for him.

'Who is it?' came the voice of the servant girl, Rhoda.

When she heard Peter reply, she was amazed. She ran to tell the others but they simply would not believe her.

'It's true – he's still knocking!' she cried.

She was so excited that she had forgotten to let him in!

They opened the door and were overjoyed to see that it *was* Peter. He told them how God had rescued him, then he slipped away somewhere safe while his friends praised God and talked together about the wonderful things he was doing for them.

PAUL THE TRAVELLER

Saul goes to Antioch

Soon the news reached the believers in Jerusalem that a church had started in a town called Antioch. The people there loved Jesus so much that they were always talking about him, and they had been given the nickname, 'the Christians'.

'This is good news,' said the church leaders in Jerusalem. 'Let's send Saul's friend Barnabas to Antioch to help the new believers to learn more about Jesus.'

'Of course I'll go,' said Barnabas. 'But I think I might need some help for this special job.' He went all the way to Tarsus to find Saul.

'Why don't you come and help me to work with the new friends of Jesus in Antioch?' he asked.

Saul agreed gladly. For a whole year Barnabas and Saul worked hard in Antioch, until one special day when God spoke to the Christians as they were praying. 'I want Saul and Barnabas to do something special for me. They must travel far away to many other countries to tell people there about Jesus,' said God.

Full of excitement, all the Christians placed their hands on the two friends and prayed for them. Then they set off on their travels. They took Barnabas' young nephew, John Mark, with them to help them in their work.

Saul and Elymas

First they sailed to the island of Cyprus where Barnabas had been born. The Roman governor gave them a warm welcome. He wanted to hear about Jesus, but a friend of his, a magician called Elymas, was standing by. He didn't want the governor to believe in Jesus and he kept interrupting Saul. This made Saul angry. He spoke sternly to Elymas.

'Stop trying to twist the truth, you trickster! Because you are setting yourself against God, you will go blind for a while!'

At once Elymas felt as though a thick fog was covering his eyes. He groped around for someone to lead him. The governor was amazed; he felt sure that Saul must be speaking the truth about Jesus.

From now on Saul began to use his Roman name of Paul. But, although he travelled to many other countries, he never forgot his own people, the Jews.

John Mark goes home

Paul and Barnabas planned to travel into Turkey. John Mark was very quiet on the voyage across from Cyprus. Once they reached the mainland he refused to go any further with them. Perhaps he was homesick, or jealous of Paul who seemed to be getting more important than his uncle, Barnabas.

Rather sadly, Paul and Barnabas went on their way over the high mountain passes to a district called Pisidia. They began to teach the Jews who lived there about Jesus. Many of them listened eagerly and the good news spread like wildfire through the surrounding villages. Even here, the Jewish leaders were angry. 'Those two travellers, Paul and Barnabas, are stirring up trouble in our town,' the leaders told some of the rich citizens, who believed them. Paul and Barnabas were thrown roughly out of the town. But they went bravely on their way. 'God is with us,' Paul said. 'There are groups of Christians everywhere now and the new Christians here will go on meeting together, even though we've been thrown out.' Paul always remembered the new Christians, even when he was far away. He prayed for them and wrote letters to encourage them.

Jupiter and Mercury

One day Paul and Barnabas came to a city called Lystra, where there was a temple to the chief Roman god, Jupiter. As Paul talked about Jesus he saw a lame man in the crowd. He felt sure that the man believed what he was saying and could be made well.

'Stand up and walk!' ordered Paul.

The man jumped to his feet immediately, completely cured.

'These men must really be gods in disguise!' shouted the crowd.

They decided that Barnabas must be Jupiter because he was the taller, and that Paul must be Mercury, the messenger of the gods, because he did the talking.

The priest of Jupiter brought flowers and bulls to offer to Paul and Barnabas. The two friends were horrified! They ran into the crowd, tearing their clothes and shouting, 'Stop! We're not gods; just ordinary people like you, come to tell you about the one true God who loves you and provides you with the good things you need to live!'

They only just managed to stop the crowd worshipping them!

Paul and Barnabas disagree

After many adventures the two friends returned home to Antioch. They had been away for two years and had travelled over a thousand miles. Because of their work, many new churches had begun.

The Christians in Antioch were overjoyed to hear that God was giving his help and power to so many new followers of Jesus.

Paul and Barnabas spent some time with them, and then they

decided to set out on another journey to visit all the new churches and see how they were getting on.

Barnabas wanted to take John Mark with them again.

'That wouldn't be right at all!' said Paul sharply. 'He didn't stick it out last time. He deserted us as soon as we set foot in Turkey and had those high mountains to cross!'

'Well, I think we should give him another chance. After all, the boy is older now . . .' began Barnabas, but Paul refused to agree.

After some argument they decided to go their different ways. Barnabas set sail for Cyprus and took John Mark with him, while Paul chose a new companion called Silas.

Two new helpers

Paul and Silas revisited the new churches in Turkey. When they reached Lystra they found everyone talking about a young man called Timothy.

'He's such a fine Christian!' they told Paul. 'His mother is Jewish and she's a Christian now, too. His father was a Greek.'

Paul listened thoughtfully.

'I'd like to meet that boy!' he said to Silas. 'We could use someone like him, who belongs to both the Jews and the Greeks!'

When Paul met Timothy he liked him at once. He asked him to join them on their travels. Timothy was delighted, even though he knew it would be difficult and dangerous. He and Paul became very fond of each other, and Paul always treated Timothy just like a son.

Before long another helper joined the three travellers – a Greek doctor called Luke. Luke turned out to be a faithful friend. He also wrote down the story of Paul's adventures which we still have in our Bibles today.

The friends go to Greece

One night, soon after he had met Luke, Paul had a dream. He saw a man from a place called Macedonia in Greece who begged him to go there to tell the Macedonians the good news of Jesus. Paul knew at once that this was what God wanted him to do. He and his friends got ready to leave immediately.

They sailed to Greece and made their way to a town called Philippi where they stayed for a few days. On the Sabbath they found a group of Jewish women praying by the river because there was no other meeting-place. Paul and Silas joined them and lost no time in telling them about Jesus.

One of the women, whose name was Lydia, believed and she was baptised. Lydia made her living selling the beautiful purple cloth which only the very rich people wore. She invited Paul and his friends to stay in her house while they were in Philippi.

Paul and Silas in prison

Trouble was in store for Paul and Silas. A poor slave girl started to follow them around. She could tell people's fortunes, and her masters earned a lot of money from people who wanted to know what their futures would be. Whenever the girl saw Paul and Silas she would call, 'Here are two servants of the most high God!'

Paul was upset by this. He knew that the girl's powers came from an evil spirit and not from God. At last he could bear it no longer. Through the power of Jesus he freed her from the evil spirit and at once her magic powers left her.

The girl's masters were furious. They wouldn't be able to earn any more money. They grabbed hold of Paul and Silas and dragged them off to the city authorities. The two friends were beaten and then chained up in prison. But they knew God was with them still and they spent the night singing hymns of praise to him.

The jailer

Suddenly, at about midnight, a violent earthquake shook the prison. Doors swung open and the chains fell off the prisoners. The jailer rushed in to find out what was happening. He was sure everyone had escaped and he drew his sword to kill himself, for he knew he would be blamed for losing the prisoners.

Paul saw what he was doing and shouted, 'Stop! Don't kill yourself! We're all here!'

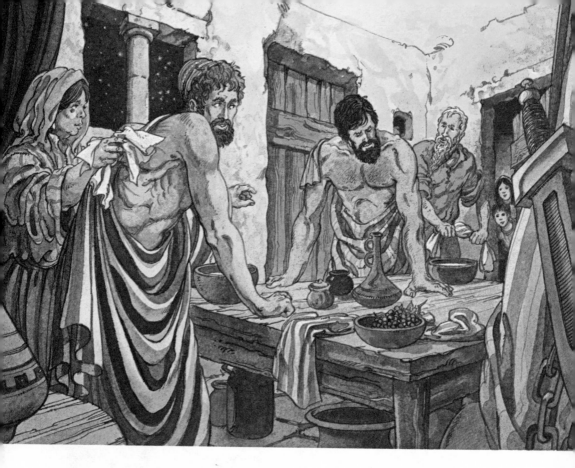

Amazed, the jailer dropped his sword and called for lights. He rushed into the cell and knelt trembling before Paul and Silas.

'What must I do now?' he asked.

They answered simply, 'Believe in Jesus and you and your family will be saved by God.'

At once the jailer took Paul and Silas to his home. He washed their wounds and they baptised him and all his family.

In the morning the authorities sent their men to the house to tell the jailer to let Paul and Silas go. To the jailer's surprise Paul was angry.

'I am a Roman citizen,' he said, 'and that means that I have special rights. A Roman citizen can't be arrested and punished without a trial, but you have beaten me and imprisoned me for no reason. Now you want me to go away and forget it. I won't go until you apologise!'

The authorities were frightened when they heard that Paul was a Roman citizen, and they apologised to him and asked him to leave the city. So, after saying goodbye to Lydia and the other new Christians, Paul and his friends travelled on to another big town called Thessalonica, seventy miles away.

Trouble in Thessalonica

They spent three weeks there, and a number of people believed their message, including some Greeks who worshipped God in the Jewish way. Some of the leading women of the town were among them, but the synagogue leaders found it hard to believe in Jesus. They were so worried and upset by this new teaching that they stirred up a whole mob against Paul and his friends.

'We must hide!' exclaimed Paul, seeing the crowd come storming along the street looking for them. Paul, Silas, Luke and Timothy slipped quietly away. The crowd hammered on every door yelling for them to come out. The only person they could find was a man called Jason, who had had Paul staying in his house.

At once they dragged him off to the rulers of the town.

'This man's an enemy of the Roman Emperor!' they shouted. 'He follows another king called Jesus!'

The rulers were furious. Jason had no chance to explain. He had to pay a large fine before they would let him go. As soon as he was free he went to find Paul and his friends and helped them to escape from the town.

119

Paul in Athens

Paul, Silas, Luke and Timothy made their way quickly to another city, Berea. The people there were friendly and listened eagerly to their teaching about Jesus. But danger still followed Paul. His enemies came after him and tried to turn the people of Berea against him. His friends said, 'You must try to get away, Paul. We'll stay and help the new Christians.'

'All right. I'll head towards the coast as though I'm going to find a ship, but really I'll go to Athens,' Paul decided.

'It's such a famous city you must speak for Jesus there,' the others agreed. 'We'll come and join you as soon as we can.'

So Paul went to Athens. While he waited for Silas and Timothy to join him there, he spent his time looking round the city. When he noticed the hundreds of statues of different gods and goddesses which the people worshipped, Paul wanted to tell them about the true God.

The Athenians enjoyed discussing ideas of all kinds, so they were interested to hear Paul. They asked him to come and talk to their city council. Paul went gladly. He told them about Jesus who had come to die so that their wrong-doings could be forgiven. He told them how God had raised Jesus from the dead. Some people believed Paul, but many of them laughed at him. They thought he was talking nonsense.

'Who is this idiot?' they asked.

Paul didn't mind. He knew that following Jesus was more important than being thought clever.

Priscilla and Aquila

Paul soon moved on to the busy port of Corinth, just north of Athens. Here he made friends with a Jew called Aquila and his wife Priscilla. Aquila was a tent maker, and as Paul had learned the same trade when he was a boy, he stayed with them and helped them with their work. Together they sat and stitched the heavy tents.

By now Silas, Timothy and Luke had rejoined Paul. They went all over Corinth, teaching the people about Jesus. They stayed there for a year and a half, talking to anyone who would listen and helping the new believers to follow Jesus in a city where most people worshipped other gods.

As usual the Jewish leaders tried to stop Paul. They went to the

Roman governor of Corinth to complain about him. This time though, the governor was on Paul's side.

'If Paul had committed a crime I would have done something about it,' he said, 'but this is something you must settle yourselves!'

So Paul was able to go on speaking freely about Jesus.

'It's been very good here,' he said one day. 'But I must get back to Jerusalem.'

'We'll come with you as far as Ephesus,' said Priscilla and Aquila. 'That's going to be our new home.'

So the friends set sail and travelled together as far as Ephesus. Paul didn't stay long there. He wanted to get back to Jerusalem as quickly as he could. He did visit one synagogue, though, and preach about Jesus there. Many of the people who heard him begged him to stay and tell them more, and Paul promised to come back.

His ship took him as far as the

large port of Caesarea close to Joppa, and from there he travelled by land to Jerusalem where the leaders of the Christians lived. He had plenty of exciting news to tell them!

Then he went home to Antioch and spent some time with his friends there.

Paul's third journey

Before long, however, he decided it was time to be travelling again. He set out to visit the new churches in the towns where he had first taught about Jesus. The Christians there were overjoyed to see him. They welcomed him warmly, and he encouraged them to be brave followers of Jesus.

At last he made his way to Ephesus as he had promised. Ephesus was a large town with a splendid temple to the goddess Diana which people came from many miles away to see. Some of the people who lived there had already become Christians, but most of them worshipped the Roman gods, and many practised

magic. They had heavy books of spells and little scrolls with charms written on them, which they used to carry with them to bring them luck.

When Paul arrived he began to teach the people about Jesus. He also healed many sick people in the name of Jesus and drove away evil spirits. Soon the people realised that Jesus was more powerful than any magic.

Some of the Christians who had practised magic realised that what they had been doing was wrong. They decided to have nothing more to do with it. Solemnly they brought their books and scrolls to the market place and made a huge bonfire. Thousands of valuable books were burnt up. News of this soon spread, and more people came to believe in Jesus because of it.

Riot in Ephesus

There were many silversmiths in Ephesus who earned money by making models of the goddess Diana and her temple. After Paul had been there three years, they grew worried.

'If things go on like this,' they grumbled, 'there'll be nobody praying to Diana any more. They'll all be following Jesus and we'll be out of a job!'

When the townspeople heard

this they were furious and they began to shout, 'Long live Diana! Long live Diana!'

They found two of Paul's friends and dragged them off to the theatre where the public meetings were held. For two hours the people chanted and shouted. Nobody could calm them down. Paul wanted to go to try, but his friends wouldn't let him. It was too dangerous. At last the town clerk managed to make himself heard.

'We all know that our goddess Diana is great and powerful. Nobody disputes that. But you have brought these men here although they have done nothing criminal. If you have any complaints, make them in the law courts. Don't get Ephesus a bad name by causing a riot!'

The crowd listened to the town clerk and went home without making any more trouble. But Paul knew it was no longer safe for him to stay there.

He left Ephesus and travelled on to visit more of the churches he had helped to start on his first journeys. Then, after several months, Paul decided to go back to Jerusalem.

Eutychus

On the way he and his friends stopped at the port of Troas. They stayed with the Christians who lived there, and on their last evening they all met together to worship God. The meeting was held in a room at the top of a tall building and it was crowded.

People sat close together on the floor or perched on the window sills. Smoky oil lamps hung from the ceiling and the air was stuffy and warm. Paul began to talk — he had so much to say before he left! One of the boys, called Eutychus, who was sitting on the window sill, began to doze. His head slipped back, and, before anyone could help him, he slid backwards through the window and crashed to the ground.

His friends rushed downstairs, but he was dead.

'Don't worry!' Paul put his arms round Eutychus as he spoke. 'Look! He's alive!'

Sure enough, Eutychus opened his eyes and then got to his feet. Overjoyed, his friends helped him upstairs again, and there they stayed until morning, praising God and listening to Paul's message.

Paul says goodbye to the Ephesians

The journey back to Jerusalem took Paul near Ephesus again, but he did not want to lose time by stopping there. Instead he sent a message to the leaders of the church asking them to meet him at the port where the boat was docked. When they arrived he spoke solemnly to them.

'I don't know what will happen to me in Jerusalem. God has warned me to expect trouble and imprisonment wherever I go, but

that doesn't worry me! All I want is to finish the work God has given me to do: telling everyone I can, the good news about Jesus. So please pray for me; and keep on following Jesus yourselves.'

Then Paul and the leaders knelt

and prayed together. Sadly they said goodbye. They knew they would never see Paul again.

Agabus' message

The ship carried Paul and his friends on across the sea. Once again they called at the port of Caesarea. This time they stayed with Philip who had baptised the Queen of Ethiopia's treasurer. He had four daughters who were all followers of Jesus.

While they were staying with Philip a man called Agabus arrived. God's Holy Spirit told him that Paul's life was in danger. Agabus tried to warn him. He took Paul's long belt and tied his own hands and feet with it.

'The Jews in Jerusalem will tie up the owner of this belt like this and then they'll hand him over to the Romans!' he said.

At once everyone begged Paul not to go to Jerusalem. Some people even had tears in their eyes as they pleaded with him to stay. But Paul said, 'You mustn't cry like that. You're breaking my heart. Don't you see that I'm ready to die for my Lord Jesus?'

They tried even harder to persuade him to change his mind, but he refused to listen. At last they gave up.

'We must leave it all to the Lord,' they said. 'He is in control; and we must do what he wants because that is best.'

PAUL THE PRISONER

Paul in danger

At last Paul reached Jerusalem. The Christians there welcomed him warmly, but they were worried for they knew Paul had many enemies there. And it was not long before his enemies attacked him.

Some of them spotted Paul in the streets with a friend from Ephesus. When they next saw Paul he was in the temple where only Jewish men were allowed to be. At once they decided that he had brought his Ephesian friend with him.

'Kill him!' they yelled. 'He's defying our sacred laws by

bringing foreigners into our most holy place!'

Paul is arrested

At once a crowd gathered and dragged Paul out of the temple. They hit and kicked him, shouting angrily as they did so. Then someone told the commander of the Roman soldiers in Jerusalem that there was a riot. Quickly he took some men and marched to the temple. He stopped the crowd beating Paul and had him arrested. The soldiers had to hoist him up on their shoulders and carry him away to keep the crowd from tearing him apart. Paul tried to explain to the crowd about Jesus, but they wouldn't listen.

The Roman commander could not understand what Paul had done to enrage the crowd. He ordered his men to beat Paul until he told them. So the soldiers stripped Paul and tied him to a post. Then Paul calmly told them that he was a Roman citizen. They were breaking the law even by tying him up without giving him a fair trial first! Anxiously the commander questioned Paul. 'I had to buy my citizenship. It cost me a lot of money!' he said.

'I was born a Roman citizen!' Paul replied quietly.

Frightened, the commander had Paul's chains taken off him.

Paul before the council

The commander still wasn't sure what Paul had done to make the Jews angry, so the next day he took Paul before the Jewish council.

Paul faced them calmly and began to explain what he had been doing.

At once the high priest ordered someone to hit him across the mouth.

Paul was angry. It was against the law to hit a prisoner.

'You hypocrite!' he shouted. 'You say that I've broken God's law but here you are doing the same yourselves!'

'Don't you know that you're talking to the high priest?' said the people standing near him.

Paul apologised. He knew that the law said that nobody should say bad things about the high priest.

'Brothers,' he called out, 'I've done nothing wrong. I'm on trial here simply because I believe that God will raise the dead to life!'

Now some of the council believed this, too, but others didn't. Both sides began to argue about what Paul had said. They grew so angry that the Roman

commander was frightened that they would tear Paul to pieces between them, and he ordered his soldiers to drag Paul to safety.

That night Paul saw Jesus standing beside his bed.

'Don't be afraid, Paul!' said Jesus. 'You have spoken bravely about me here in Jerusalem, and you must do the same in Rome, too!'

Paul's greatest wish had always been to speak for Jesus in Rome, the great city where the Emperor ruled. Now, perhaps through this trouble, his wish would be fulfilled. In spite of everything he felt happy.

The plot

'Paul thinks he's safe now he's with the Romans, but we'll get him yet,' muttered his enemies. They vowed not to eat or drink until they had killed him.

'We'll ask the chief priests to

send Paul to them for further questioning, and we'll kill him on the way there,' they plotted.

They didn't see the little boy who crouched in the shadows and heard every word. He was Paul's nephew! Quietly he slipped away to the fort to warn his uncle.

At once Paul called an officer who took the boy to the commander.

The commander led the boy to a quiet corner.

'What do you have to tell me, son?' he asked.

When he heard the boy's story he sent him home, telling him not to breathe a word to anyone. Then he ordered two hundred foot soldiers, seventy horsemen and two hundred spearmen to get ready to take Paul out of Jerusalem as soon as it got dark.

'Take him down to Caesarea and let Governor Felix deal with the case!'

The commander wrote a letter to Felix about Paul: 'The Jews were about to kill this man, but I found out that he was a Roman citizen, so I stepped in to save his life. He seems to have broken some Jewish

law. I can't find him guilty of any crime against Rome. The Jews are still plotting against him, so I am sending him to you.'

It wasn't quite the truth, but it would never do for Governor Felix to find out that he had put a Roman citizen in chains and nearly had him beaten!

Paul left Jerusalem safely, surrounded by armed men. He knew God was looking after him.

Paul goes before Felix

Five days later the high priest and other Jewish leaders hurried to Caesarea to tell Felix their side of the story.

'We want your excellency to know that the prisoner Paul is a most dangerous man. He has travelled all over the Empire starting riots among the Jews,' they said. 'He came to Jerusalem, but we arrested him in the temple when he was about to stir up more trouble there.'

'I went to the temple to pray, not to start trouble!' replied Paul. 'I worship God, just as these men do, but I follow Jesus, too. I am on trial here because I tell everyone that God raised Jesus from the dead.'

Felix decided to take an easy way out. 'I'll hear Paul's case later!' he said.

He hoped, too, that if he left Paul in prison for long enough Paul would give him some money in order to be set free. So Felix never gave Paul another trial. He kept him closely guarded, but allowed his friends to visit him.

The new governor

At last, after two whole years, a new governor took over from Felix. The new governor, whose name was Festus, wanted to please the Jews, so he asked Paul to go to Jerusalem for another trial. Paul knew he would be killed if he set foot in the city.

'I am a Roman citizen,' Paul pleaded. 'I've done nothing wrong. There's no truth in any of the charges the Jewish leaders have brought against me. I want the Roman Emperor to try me. I appeal to have my case transferred to Rome!'

This was one of Paul's rights as a citizen, and Festus had to agree.

While arrangements were being made for Paul's journey, the king and queen of Judea arrived to welcome the new governor. Festus told them about Paul, and the king, Agrippa, asked to see him. The whole court gathered to hear his story. Eagerly, Paul told them all he had done to tell people everywhere about Jesus. 'Jesus is the special king God promised to us. He had to be punished and die, but God raised him from death,' he explained, but Festus interrupted: 'You're mad, Paul!' he cried, but King Agrippa wasn't so sure.

He talked to Paul a little longer, then he turned to Festus.

'If Paul hadn't appealed to Caesar you could have set him free,' he said. 'He has done nothing wrong.'

Paul sets sail

It was late summer when Paul set sail for Rome, guarded by an officer called Julius. Two of Paul's friends, Luke and Aristarchus, travelled with him.

Julius could see that Paul was a good man, different from the

beginning to blow when they set out again. Once they reached Crete, Paul advised the ship's captain not to sail any further until winter was over.

However, both Julius and the captain were anxious to get to

dangerous criminals he often had to guard. He treated Paul well, and when the ship called at a port called Sidon, where Paul had friends, he allowed him to go to visit them. They were glad to see Paul, and gave him all sorts of useful things for the long voyage to Italy.

The autumn winds were

Rome, and they decided to press on with the journey.

Hardly had they left harbour when a furious storm blew up. The ship was thrown in all directions. Desperately the crew threw the cargo overboard to make the boat lighter, but still they could not get her under control. For two weeks they were driven by the storm.

Only Paul had any hope that they would be kept safe.

'God told me in a dream that we shall all reach Rome,' he said. 'I must stand my trial before Caesar. The ship will be lost, but God will protect us all.'

On the fourteenth night the sailors guessed that they were close to land. Frightened in case the ship drifted on to rocks, they dropped anchor and waited for dawn. Paul urged them to rest and eat. When they saw how calm he was, they were encouraged and had some food.

The first glimmer of dawn showed them a stretch of unknown coastline. Carefully the sailors tried to guide the boat towards the shore.

They didn't see the sandbank that blocked their way until the ship struck it! The boat was held fast while the pounding waves battered the stern.

The soldiers wanted to kill Paul and some other prisoners on board to stop them escaping in the confusion, but Julius stopped them. He ordered those who could swim to jump overboard and make for the shore. The rest were to use the broken planks from the ship as floats.

So it was that, as Paul had promised, everyone arrived safely on dry land.

Paul and the snake

Once ashore they discovered that they were on the island of Malta. The weather was cold and it started to rain. The kindly islanders lit a huge bonfire for them, and Paul got busy gathering sticks. He was about to throw a bundle of wood on to the fire when a snake, brought out by the heat, coiled itself around his hand.

The islanders watched, horrified. 'This man is obviously a murderer! He's managed to escape the shipwreck, but he's doomed to die for his crimes,' they said.

But Paul shook the snake off and it fell into the fire. The islanders waited for him to swell up or drop dead, poisoned; when he didn't, they were very impressed. 'He must be a god,' they decided.

The governor's father

It so happened that the island's chief official, a man called Publius, lived near the beach

142

where Paul and the others landed. Publius welcomed them warmly and invited them to stay with him, even though his father lay at home unwell.

'God rescued us, I'm sure he will cure your father!' Paul said.

He laid his hands on the old man and prayed. Publius' father recovered at once. The news spread all over Malta and many sick people came to Paul to be cured.

More impressed than ever, the grateful islanders brought Paul presents. When he set sail again, three months later, they loaded the ship with all sorts of useful things to replace what had been lost in the storm.

Paul and his friends reached Italy without any more adventures. They landed in a busy port and began the long journey to Rome by road. The news of their arrival reached the Christians in Rome, and they hurried out of the city to meet them. Paul was delighted at the welcome they gave him, and thanked God for bringing him to them safely.

Paul was still a prisoner. He was allowed to live in a rented house, but he had a soldier with him all the time to guard him. He could not leave the house, but many people came to visit him. He wrote letters to his friends in the many places he had visited, helping them with their problems, and encouraging them to follow the way of Jesus wherever they were.

PAUL'S LETTERS

Onesimus

'Master! Your runaway slave, Onesimus, has come back!' a breathless messenger rushed up to Paul's friend, Philemon. 'He's come all the way from Rome with a letter from Paul!'

'And what does he expect to get from me?' shouted Philemon angrily. 'A runaway slave deserves to be put to death. Bring him here at once!'

Onesimus came in, holding out a letter from Paul. Philemon broke the seal and unrolled the scroll. Suddenly he remembered the words of Jesus: 'Forgive those who wrong you...' Philemon was a follower of Jesus and many Christians who lived nearby came to worship God in his beautiful home. His anger began to cool.

'Brother Philemon,' wrote Paul. 'I thank God for you every time I pray.' Philemon softened. He read on.

'Onesimus has become a Christian too. He is like a son to me now. He has been a great help to me in prison. I should like to keep him here to help me, but he belongs to you. If he has stolen anything I will pay it back. You see, he is much more than a slave to you now. He is a Christian brother. Please welcome him back, just as if he were me. I am sure you will do what I ask; in fact I know you will do even more.'

Philemon thought of Paul chained up in prison. He reread the letter thoughtfully. Finally he turned to Onesimus waiting quietly beside him. 'Welcome home!' he said, and held out his arms.

Parents and children

'Children,' Paul wrote in one of his letters, 'obey your parents. It's the right thing to do. It is one of the commandments God gave long ago and it has a promise to go with it. "If you obey your parents all will go well with you."

'Parents,' he continued, 'don't

nag at your children or keep threatening them. You will only make them resentful and angry. Instead, bring them up lovingly with positive suggestions. Correct them when it's necessary. Above all, teach them about Jesus.'

The great race

Paul watched from his window. In the street, a crowd cheered a young athlete who had just won a race. On his head was his prize — a crown of green leaves. Paul thought about the races he had watched when he was free. He remembered how eagerly the athletes tried to win crowns, training for months beforehand, thinking about nothing but the games.

Smiling to himself, Paul went back to the letter he was writing.

'Following Jesus is like running a race in the arena,' he wrote. 'I don't want to be disqualified or left behind. I press on, running hard to win the prize which God will give me. His prize doesn't wither and fade like a crown of leaves. It lasts for ever. His prize is being with Jesus and sharing in his glory. You must run this race, too. Get into training now, and run well to win the prize.'

A letter to Timothy

Paul had been in prison a long time. Some of his friends deserted him. Some left him to work in other cities. Only Luke stayed with him. Paul longed to see his old friends. He wrote to his young helper, Timothy, who was working in Ephesus.

'Do your best to come to see me, and get Mark to come with you, too, because I know he will help me. Call in at Troas for the cloak I left there: it gets cold here in Rome in the winter! And bring my books and papers so that I can keep on working in prison. My life is nearly over. I have run the race, and I am waiting for my prize.'

When the letter arrived, Timothy read it quickly, glad to be of use to the old man he loved. As soon as he could, he collected his belongings and set off to find Mark, so that they could make the long journey to Rome together.

THE WORK GOES ON

The Christians in Rome

The soldier who guarded Paul sat in a corner of the busy lamplit room. As usual, all kinds of people crowded in to worship Jesus. Jews and Romans, Greeks and Asians, men, women, children and slaves all mixed freely together. The soldier had never seen anything like it before. He listened while they sang. 'Jesus died a cruel death on the cross,' they began softly. Their voices grew louder: 'But God raised him high. The whole world will bow before him because Jesus is the Lord who brings glory to God the Father.'

Their song echoed into the corners of the shadowy room, loud and triumphant.

'They must be able to hear it all over Rome,' thought the soldier. 'Soon everyone will know about this Jesus.'

He was right. Before long crowds would hear men, women and children singing praises to Jesus as they were led out to die for him, only thirty years after he himself had died and risen again. Paul himself would be among those who died, but the lessons he had taught about Jesus were to spread through the whole world.

JOHN'S VISION

John sees Jesus

Many Christians besides Paul were punished for being followers of Jesus. John, the fisherman who had been Jesus' friend when he was alive on Earth, was arrested by the Romans and sent away to live on the small island of Patmos. John was old now, and although the island looked lovely when the sun shone and ripened the grapes on the steep green hillsides, it was hard to live there alone. He could not see his friends or meet with other Christians to worship Jesus with them.

In spite of his troubles John still loved and worshipped the Lord Jesus. One day, when he was praying, God spoke to John. He heard a voice ring out behind him like a trumpet.

John turned round and saw Jesus standing close by, surrounded by seven golden candlesticks. His face shone like the sun, and his whole body blazed with light. In his right hand he held seven stars. John fell down at his feet.

'Don't be afraid,' Jesus said. 'I am the One who was there in the beginning and I shall still be there at the end of time. I was dead but now I am alive for ever.'

His voice flooded the quiet island like the roar of a foaming waterfall. 'These seven stars and the seven candlesticks stand for the churches in seven places. I have a message for each church. Write down everything you hear and see.'

So John wrote it all down.

First John wrote messages to the seven churches, just as Jesus gave him the words.

'I know you haven't given up your faith,' he wrote to the first church, 'even though you have been badly treated. But some of you don't love me as much as you used to, and you've started to do wrong. Stop doing wrong and listen to my Holy Spirit. There is a beautiful tree in God's garden and I give its fruit to the people who win a victory for me.'

Jesus spoke to the other churches in the same way, warning them to be obedient and faithful so that they could share in his victory and joy.

He spoke sternly to the seventh church: 'You think you are strong and powerful and rich, but really you are weak and poor because you don't rely on me. Turn back to me. I shall give you everything you need. Look, I'm just outside your door. Can't you hear me knocking? Open the door and let me in, and we shall sit and enjoy a meal together.'

God as King

After this, God showed John what heaven is like. A door stood

wide open and John saw a royal throne. Someone sat there, someone whose face shone as though it were made of precious jewels. A rainbow curved round the throne, the person on the throne was so glorious and powerful that all John could see was dazzling flashes of lightning. He heard an endless rumble of thunder. He looked down and saw seven fiery torches flaming around the throne, reflected in a million darting gold pieces by what seemed to be a sea of purest glass stretching out in front of the throne.

Magnificent beings bowed before the throne where God sat. They sang all day and all night, never stopping, 'Holy, holy, holy is the Lord God, the only ruler of the world from before its beginning to beyond its end.'

Twenty four leaders took off their golden crowns and tossed them down in front of God, as a sign that he was their king. The singing went on and on, an endless 'thank you' to God. As John listened, he knew that no matter how hard the Roman Emperor or other rulers tried to hurt Christians, God really was in control and he always would be.

John wrote down everything that he heard and saw. He knew that the churches that were being attacked for worshipping Jesus would be made brave when they read how powerful and wonderful God is.

The new Jerusalem

Finally, God showed John a new heaven and a new Earth.

He heard God's voice saying, 'Look, I am making everything new!' and he saw a beautiful bride on her way to her wedding. 'All the old sad things have vanished,' said the voice. 'God will wipe away your tears and dry your eyes. There is no death now, no sadness or crying or hurt.'

'Come, John,' said the angel. 'I will show you the bride whom Jesus loves.'

The angel took John to the top of a mountain and he saw a city just like Jerusalem, all lit up and shining, filled with God's glory. There was no temple there because God himself was in the middle of the city and Jesus was with him, brighter than the golden streets.

152

'I am the bright morning star,' said Jesus. 'I am coming soon.'

There was no night-time at all in the city, and its gates stayed wide open.

'Come,' said the bride, whose wedding party is for everyone.

'Come,' repeated the Holy Spirit, who helped John to see heaven.

'Come,' wrote John. 'Everyone come. Are you thirsty? Jesus is like a drink of cold water. Come, then, because all this is true, and Jesus says he is coming soon.

'Come soon, come very soon, Lord Jesus!' John finished his book.

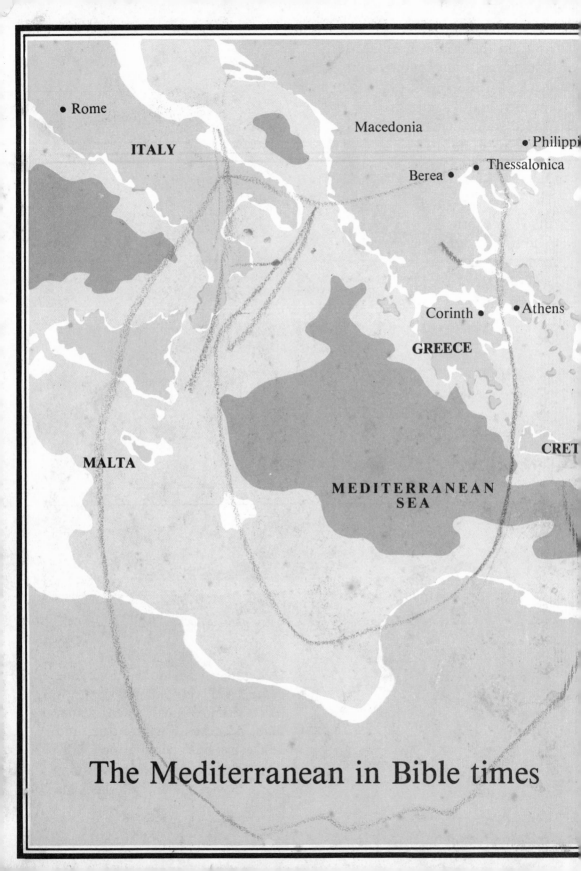

The Mediterranean in Bible times